MAKING THE MOST OF MEAT

A New Zealand Cookbook
Jan Bilton

Whitcoulls Publishers
Christchurch London

Cover photo: Peppered Rump Steak

Thanks to R. & W. Hellaby Ltd for the use of transparencies and other materials.

First published by R. & W. Hellaby Ltd in 1978
Revised and updated by Whitcoulls Publishers in 1985

©1985 Jan Bilton

Whitcoulls Publishers
Christchurch, New Zealand

All rights reserved. No part of this publication may be reproduced, stored in a retrieval system, or transmitted in any form·or by any means, electronic, mechanical, photocopying, recording or otherwise, without prior written permission of the publishers.

ISBN 0 7233 0733 4

Typeset by Quickset Platemakers Ltd
Christchurch
Printed in Singapore

CONTENTS

Introduction	4
The Boiling Method	7
Better Braising	10
Microwave Cooking	13
Countless Casseroles	18
Roasting the Right Way	23
Frying and Grilling those Tender Cuts	29
A Fast Grill	30
The Art of Pan Frying	34
Frying Time	38
Oriental Cooking	41
Fun Fondues	45
Barbecues for Outdoor Living	48
Pressure Cooking	52
Variety Meats	55
Mince Magic	61
Serving Sausages Differently	66
Pies-a-Plenty	70
Curries	74
Making the Most of Leftovers	78
Ham and Bacon	81
Continental Meats	86
Home Freezing and Storage	91
Glossary	96
Cuts of Meat	98
Index	100

INTRODUCTION

Over the years, recipe books have been produced on every imaginable facet of the culinary art. They come in all shapes and sizes and range from the very expensive, featuring chefs of international renown, to pamphlets supporting particular products.

So why produce another one?

Making the Most of Meat is designed to provide valuable assistance in placing meat, which has received so much attention in the production and processing stages, on the table in its most tantalising and appetising form.

Meat is an excellent source of all the ingredients necessary to keep the body in good running order. Besides being enjoyable to eat, it is a powerhouse packed with protein, minerals and vitamins, all essential for building new and repairing old body tissue, and regulating body processes.

The protein of meat is of a very high quality. Meat is a good source of iron, calcium and phosphorus, necessary for healthy blood and strong bones. All the B vitamins are in meat too, and the body uses up a fresh supply of B vitamins daily.

Because it is one of the most completely digestible and utilised foods, it can appear on everyone's menu. And for slimmers! — lean meat is low in fat and fattening carbohydrates. It is satisfying too, curbing the desire to nibble.

We all should aim for a well balanced diet — with meat on the menu you are off to a good start.

BUYING MEAT

When buying meat, it is important to look for:
- good colour with no dark or discoloured patches
- firm white fat, which is not oily
- fresh smell.

When considering the amount to buy, the following are general rules:
- boneless meat — allow 100–170 g per person
- meat with average amount of bone — allow 170–280 g per person
- meat with a large amount of bone — allow 280–340 g per person
- chops (small) — allow 2 per person
- chops (large) — allow 1 per person

WEIGHTS AND MEASURES

Where possible, cup and spoon measurements have been used in the recipes instead of weights. This allows the use of your current measuring cup and spoons, whether they be metric, British Standard or American. It is important to use the same type of measurements consistently throughout one recipe.

Grams to ounces
Approximate conversions to nearest 5 g

g	25	50	75	100	125	150	175	200	225	275	350	400	450
oz	1	2	3	3½	4	5	6	7	8	10	12	14	16

1 kg (one kilogram) = 1000 g = 2 lb 4 oz
0.5 kg (½ kilo) = 500 g = 1 lb 2 oz

Liquid measurements
The metric cup is one-tenth larger than the American standard (8 oz) cup

1 tablespoon 15 ml
1 cup 250 ml
1 litre 1000 ml

Centimetres to inches

cm	2.5	5	18	20	23	25
in	1	2	7	8	9	10

Temperatures

	very cool	cool	moderate	hot	very hot
Gas	¼ ½ 1	2 3	4 5	6 7 8	9 10
Elect. °C	110 120 140	150 160	180 190	200 220 230	250 260
°F	225 250 275	300 325	350 375	400 425 450	475 500

Abbreviations

- g   gram
- kg   kilogram
- °C   degree Celsius
- mm   millimetre
- cm   centimetre
- ml   millilitre
- l   litre
- t   teaspoon
- T   tablespoon
- D   dessertspoon

Mutton Ham

THE BOILING METHOD

The aroma of pickled pork bubbling in the pot invites taste buds to take action. Pickled or corned meat adds variety to the menu because of its flavour and method of cookery. The term is actually a misnomer — *boiling* is spoiling; simmering is best.

The corned meat is placed in a pan with sufficient cold water to cover. Putting it straight into boiling water causes shrinkage of the meat and loss of flavour. Seasonings such as sugar, spices, herbs and vegetables may be added. The pan is covered and slowly brought to boiling point. Whole root vegetables can be added near the end of the cooking time and served with the hot meat. The water used to cook the meat can be kept as a base for soups or stews. If preferred, soak the corned meat in cold water for a few hours before cooking to remove some of its saltiness.

Cuts of meat which may be boiled

BEEF	VEAL	LAMB/ MUTTON	TRADITIONAL PORK
corned silverside	knuckles	leg	(pickled or corned)
corned brisket		shoulder	forequarter
tongue		tongue	belly
shin			hock
			hand

MUTTON HAM

Sometimes called smoked mutton or Scotch ham, mutton ham is a tasty substitute for the genuine ham. A leg of mutton is corned then transferred to a smokehouse where it acquires its smoky flavour from burning manuka.

1 smoked mutton ham　　**2 onions**
6 peppercorns　　　　　　**4 cloves**
1 bayleaf

Soak mutton ham in bucket of water overnight. Drain and place in large pan.

Cover meat with water, add seasonings, cover pan and slowly bring to the boil. Simmer 30 minutes per 500 g. Allow to cool in cooking liquid.

Skin may be removed and a glaze brushed over the meat.

BRAWN

Serves 8-10

A variety of meats are boiled, chopped finely then set in aspic. This recipe uses pickled pork, gravy beef and veal. Pig's head brawn can be made in a similar manner — remove the eyes before cooking.

500 g pickled pork	2 t mixed herbs
500 g gravy beef	½ cup vinegar
2 pieces veal knuckle	2 t Worcestershire sauce
Salt	1 T gelatine
3 cloves	2 T water
1 bayleaf	

Place meat in large saucepan and cover with water. Add seasonings. Cover and bring to the boil. Simmer about 3 hours or until meat comes away from bones. Allow to cool. Remove excess fat from surface. Dice meat finely and pack into a greased mould, such as a 23 x 13 cm loaf tin.

Place 2 cups strained stock into a saucepan, add vinegar and sauce. Soften gelatine in the 2 T water and dissolve in hot stock. Strain and pour over meat in mould so that it is just covered. Refrigerate until set firmly. Unmould onto serving dish and serve sliced with salad vegetables.

CANTERBURY MUTTON

A substitute for a ham, a leg of mutton weighs about 4 kg. It may be glazed in a similar manner to a ham. The leg is corned but unlike mutton ham is not smoked. Hogget, lamb or fresh mutton may be used.

1 corned leg mutton/hogget	2 T golden syrup
1 rasher bacon	1 carrot
2 large onions	3 sprigs parsley
8 cloves	

Soak meat for 2-3 hours before cooking if desired. Drain. Place meat in a large pan and cover with water. Add bacon (or bacon rinds), onions studded with cloves, golden syrup, carrot and parsley. Slowly bring to boil, removing any surface scum. Cover and simmer 40 minutes per 500 g.

Serve hot with mustard sauce or allow to cool completely in cooking liquid. The leg may be brushed with a mixture of ½ cup pineapple juice and 3 T brown sugar, which has been simmered for 10 minutes.

LAGER BEEF

Serves about 8
Boil corned beef in beer; serve hot with chive sauce, or cold for picnics. Brisket is the economy cut.

2 kg corned silverside or brisket	**Chive Sauce**
2 cups beer	3 T butter
Water	3 T flour
2 carrots, chopped	1¼ cups stock, strained
1 clove garlic, crushed	¼ cup cream
2 onions, peeled	3-4 T finely chopped chives
4 cloves	
1 bayleaf	
8 peppercorns	

Soak beef in cold water for several hours before cooking if desired. Drain. Place meat in a large, heavy saucepan, pour in beer and enough water to cover meat. Bring to the boil and remove any surface scum.

Add carrots, garlic, 1 onion sliced, 1 whole onion studded with the 4 cloves, bayleaf and peppercorns. Reduce heat so meat just simmers. Cook 30 minutes per 500 g or until tender. If meat is to be served cold, allow to cool in cooking liquid.

To make sauce, melt butter and stir in flour. Slowly pour in stock, then add cream. Bring sauce to boil, stirring constantly. Simmer 10 minutes. Stir in chives and serve.

PICKLED PORK WITH MUSTARD SAUCE

Serves about 6
Pork cuts from the foreloin and the belly are sometimes brined or pickled.

1.5 kg piece pickled pork	**Mustard Sauce**
6 small whole onions	1 egg
2 stalks celery, chopped	¼ cup sugar
6 peppercorns	1 T flour
1 bayleaf	2 t dry mustard
¼ cup sugar	1 cup cooking liquid (from pork)
	2-4 T vinegar

Soak meat in cold water for several hours if desired. Drain. Place meat in a large saucepan. Cover with fresh cold water and add onions, celery, bayleaf and sugar. Cover and simmer 25 minutes per 500 g plus 25 minutes extra. If meat is to be served cold, allow to cool in cooking liquid.

To make sauce, beat egg and sugar. Add flour and mustard then gradually stir in cooking liquid. Cook over low heat until thickened. Serve hot.

BETTER BRAISING

This method of cooking cheaper and lean cuts of meat makes tasty, old-fashioned sense. Braising is a combination of roasting, stewing and steaming. The meat is left in one piece to prevent it drying out. It is browned in oil or fat first, then placed on a bed of sautéed chopped vegetables, such as onions and carrots. This is called a *mirepoix*. A little liquid is added and the meat is cooked in a heavy-based saucepan or in a covered pan in the oven.

When large cuts of roasting size are braised, this is called 'pot roasting'. If a *mirepoix* is not used to hold the meat, a rack in the base of a saucepan is suitable.

Cuts of meat which may be braised

BEEF
topside
thickflank
top rump
chuck roast
brisket (fresh)
rolled rib roast
prime rib roast
blade steak
bolar

VEAL
fillet (topside, thickflank, or bolar)
rolled rib roast

TRADITIONAL PORK
foreloin chops
rolled belly
leg chops
fillet

LAMB/MUTTON
rolled flap
shoulder chops
mutton leg
shanks

TRIM PORK
Y-bone steaks
scotch fillet
medallion
mid-loin steaks
butterfly steaks
rump steaks
topside roast

BRAISED PORK IN SOY SAUCE

Serves 3-4
Serve hot with rice and vegetables, or cold as a picnic meat.

500 g pork fillets
2 T oil
6 T soy sauce
6 T water
3 T dry white wine

1 t sugar
2 cloves garlic, crushed
2 t finely chopped root ginger
Pepper

In a heavy pan, sauté fillets in oil until brown on all sides. Combine all remaining ingredients and pour over meat. Cover and simmer gently for 1 hour — do not overcook. Slice and serve.

PINEAPPLE POT ROAST

Serves about 6

Pineapple-flavoured veal is a treat! Without the pineapple this is a basic pot roast recipe.

1.3 kg rolled veal pot roast	2 T fat or oil
3 T flour	220 g can pineapple slices
½ t basil	1 T Worcestershire sauce
1 t salt	Rind and juice of 1 lemon
1 clove garlic	2 T firmly packed brown sugar

Roll pot roast in flour, basil and salt. Peel and slice garlic into slivers and insert into meat. Heat oil in a heavy pan or casserole and brown meat on all sides. Drain pineapple, reserving juice. Combine pineapple juice, Worcestershire sauce, lemon rind and juice and brown sugar. Pour over meat.

Cover and cook 160°C for 2¼ hours, or simmer gently on top of range. Baste occasionally. During last 10 minutes of cooking, top with pineapple slices. Serve with potato, pineapple slices and a green vegetable.

BOLAR POT ROAST

Serves 8

This recipe is also ideal for other large beef cuts suitable for braising such as topside.

2 kg piece of bolar	4-5 medium onions, chopped
4 T flour	4-5 medium carrots, chopped
1 T dry mustard	1 t mixed herbs
1 t salt	1 cup dry white wine or water
4 T fat or oil	

Rub bolar with combined flour, mustard and salt. In a large heavy saucepan heat fat or oil. Brown meat slowly on all sides then place to one side. Roll onions and carrots in any remaining flour mixture. Sauté in fat. Place meat on top of browned vegetables, sprinkle with mixed herbs and add wine or water.

Cover and cook gently for about 3-4 hours (35 minutes per 500 g). Add extra water if necessary. Serve with vegetables and any juices as gravy.

Meat may also be cooked in a covered pan in the oven. Place vegetables on base of pan or casserole, top with meat, seasonings and wine. Cover and cook 160°C for 3-4 hours.

HERBED LAMB SHANKS

Serves 4

Mutton shanks take twice as long to cook as lamb shanks. Use oven to bake potatoes or pumpkin at the same time.

4 small lamb shanks	1 sprig parsley
2 T flour	6 black peppercorns
1 t dry mustard	1 T white vinegar
Salt	2 T tomato sauce
1 T oil	1 cup dry white wine
8 small whole onions, peeled	1 T sugar
1 large sprig rosemary	

Roll shanks in combined flour, mustard and salt. Heat oil in heavy casserole or baking dish and sauté onions. Place shanks in casserole along with all other ingredients. Cover and bake 160°C for 2 hours.

CITRUS BRAISED CHOPS

Serves 4

Cook gently to prevent scorching. The citrus fruits give a marmalade tang to the meat.

4 lamb/hogget shoulder chops	2 T water
1 T fat or oil	2 T brown sugar
1 large lemon	½ t salt
1 large orange	½ t ground ginger
4 T white vinegar	

Brown chops on both sides in fat, in a large heavy pan. Remove to one side. Drain any excess fat.

Cut lemon in 4 thick slices and place in pan. Top with browned chops, and the orange sliced into 4. Combine remaining ingredients and pour over meat. Cover, simmer gently for about 1 hour or until tender. Add a little more water if necessary during cooking. May also be cooked in oven if desired.

MICROWAVE COOKING

Microwave ovens are a great advantage for the cook in a hurry. Meat from the microwave is generally full of flavour and juice. Once the basics are mastered, cooking meat becomes effortless.

Hints
- Factors affecting the cooking times of meat: tenderness, starting temperature, thickness or shape of meat, power setting, personal preference.
- Meats are best defrosted before cooking.
- Because microwave cooking is so fast, foods do not colour up as much as in conventional cooking. Some meat dishes may therefore need to have some colour added, by being brushed with soy sauce, or sprinkled with paprika, dry brown gravy mix or special microwave browning mixes. Natural browning of meat begins after about 12 minutes of cooking.
- Boneless meat cooks less rapidly but more evenly than bony meat. Bone located near the surface of the meat reflects the microwaves into the meat so these areas cook more quickly.
- Remember that after foods are removed from the microwave they continue to cook. Allow meat to stand for one-third of the cooking time, tented loosely with foil. The internal temperature will rise 2–3°C. Your vegetables can be cooking in the microwave in the meantime.
- Stand roasts on a special microwave roasting rack or on an upturned plate. This allows juices to run to the base of the roasting dish and meat will cook more evenly.
- Tender cuts of meat are more suitable for roasting or cooking on high. Less tender cuts may be cooked successfully in variable power microwave ovens or on defrost.

ROASTING GUIDE

Meat	Power level	Cooking time per 500 g*	Internal temperature
Beef:			
Sirloin/Scotch Fillet	Full power	5 minutes	60°C
Topside	Full or half power	7 minutes 14 minutes	70°C
Pot roast	Half power	20 minutes	75°C

*Allow 2 minutes extra cooking time for every cup of sauce or other ingredient.

Lamb:

Leg	Full power	10 minutes	75°C
Forequarter	Half power	20 minutes	75°C

Pork:

	Full power	9 minutes	80°C
	Half power	18 minutes	

Veal:

Rolled Veal	Half power	20 minutes	75°C

If required, roasts may start on high power and midway through cooking power may be reduced to half. Calculate this way:
Roast topside 1 kg = 14 minutes cooking on high
or   7 minutes cooking on high and
        14 minutes cooking on half power

VEAL, APRICOT AND BANANA CASSEROLE

Serves 4

Use this recipe as a guide to preparing other casseroles in the microwave.

500 g stewing veal
1 T oil or butter
1 large chopped onion
½ t oregano
Dash of salt and pepper

1 T flour
300 g can apricot pieces
1 T lemon juice
1 banana

Cut veal into 1.5 cm cubes. Heat oil in 3-litre casserole and brown meat quickly (conventionally or in a browning dish). Add onion and seasonings and cook in microwave, uncovered, for 5 minutes. (The meat cooks more quickly without the liquid.)
   Stir in flour, apricots and lemon juice. Cover and cook on half power 25-30 minutes. Add sliced banana, cover and stand 10 minutes.

POT ROAST OF BEEF

Serves 4-6
Beef, veal, pork or lamb pot roasts can be cooked in a similar manner.

- 1 kg rolled rib roast
- 2 T butter or oil
- 1 t dried mixed herbs
- 2 medium onions, halved
- 2 carrots, chopped
- ½ cup stock
- 2 T flour

Sauté beef in butter or oil in a conventional frypan or suitable casserole, until golden on all sides. Place meat on vegetables in 3-litre casserole. Cover and cook on high 3 minutes, then on half power for 40 minutes (20 minutes per 500 g). Turn halfway during cooking.

Place cooked meat and vegetables on a warm platter and tent with foil while making gravy. Add stock mixed with flour (or cornflour) to casserole and cook about 1½ minutes until thick. Stir well.

LAMB CHOPS WITH HERBS

Serves 4
Trim excess fat from chops and snip around the outside edge to prevent chops from curling during cooking. When cooking uneven shapes such as chops, place thicker end to outside of dish as the microwave oven cooks from the outside edge to the inside.

- 4-8 lamb loin chops (500 g)
- Powdered gravy mix or browning agent
- 2 T butter
- 1 T flour
- 1 T finely chopped fresh herbs, or 1 t mixed dried herbs

Sprinkle chops with gravy mix. Melt butter in a large shallow casserole 30 seconds. Add flour and herbs. Arrange chops in casserole with meaty portions to outside of dish. Cover with waxed paper. Microwave 2 minutes. Turn chops over and cook 5 minutes. Cover (with foil) and stand 3 minutes before serving.

ROAST LEG OF LAMB

Serves 4-6

Follow this procedure when cooking roasts of meat other than lamb. Tender cuts may be roasted on high (see the roasting guide). Use other herbs and spices to complement the type of meat being cooked.

1 kg leg of lamb (approx.)
Redcurrant jelly

Powdered browning agent

Shield shank of lamb with foil to cover about 5 cm of the meat. Score fat and brush with warmed redcurrant jelly. Place meat fat side down on a roasting rack or inverted plate in a baking dish. Sprinkle with dry brown gravy mix or special microwave browning agent and cover loosely with waxed paper.

Cook 10 minutes per 500 g on full power or 20 minutes per 500 g on half power. Turn meat over halfway through cooking, baste again with jelly and sprinkle with browning agent — remove foil.

After cooking allow to stand for one-third of cooking time, loosely tented with foil.

SWEET 'N' SOUR PORK

Serves 4

Pork must be lean for this recipe. Frying veal or lean lamb can also be used.

500 g lean pork
300 g can pineapple chunks (sweetened)
¼ cup cider vinegar
1 T cornflour

2 T soy sauce
2 T oil
4 spring onions, sliced diagonally
1 green pepper, diced

Cut pork into 5 mm strips. Drain pineapple, reserving syrup. Combine syrup with vinegar and cornflour in a bowl. Heat 1 minute on high, stir, then cook a further 1 minute until thickened.

Combine pork with soy sauce, stirring to coat well. Heat oil in large shallow baking dish for 2 minutes. Stir in pork and cook on high 4 minutes, uncovered, stirring once (spoon inside mixture to outside to help meat to cook evenly). Add spring onions, green pepper and pineapple and cook 2 minutes. Stir in sauce and reheat 1-2 minutes.

Roast Leg of Lamb

DAD'S MEAT LOAF

Serves 4

Use a food processor to combine the ingredients, or mix well in a large mixing bowl. Sprinkle with browning agent after cooking if required, or sprinkle with breadcrumbs.

- 1 onion, quartered
- 1 clove garlic
- 1 stalk celery, chopped
- 1 small green pepper
- 500 g lean minced beef
- 1 cup fresh breadcrumbs
- 1 t ginger
- 1 egg
- 2 T soy sauce
- 2 T chilli sauce

Place onion, garlic, celery and green pepper into food processor and chop finely. Add all other ingredients and combine well. Shape into a loaf and place in loaf pan or onto suitable baking dish. Cook on half power for 18 minutes.

COUNTLESS CASSEROLES

Casseroles are a delight to anyone wishing to serve tasty dinners with no last minute panic. Tougher cuts of meats are usually cubed and cooked in tightly covered casseroles at a low temperature for a long time.

Stewing is similar, except that the meat is simmered in a saucepan on top of the range. Stews require more attention during cooking to prevent food from 'catching' on the base of the pan. Most recipes in this section can be cooked in casseroles, saucepans or crockpots. But remember, 'a stew boiled is a stew spoiled'.

Conserve fuel by cooking double the quantity needed and reserving half for a later date. Cook vegetables and desserts in the oven at the same time. Potatoes, kumaras and pumpkin take about 1¼ hours to bake at 180°C. Carrots, celery, broccoli, asparagus, frozen vegetables and others can be cooked in an hour in a covered casserole — add a little water, salt, pepper and butter.

Hints
- The longer and slower the cooking, the more mellow the flavour. Temperatures suggested below are the maximum — if the heat is reduced then the cooking time must be increased.
- To retain as much flavour as possible choose a casserole dish just slightly bigger than the amount of food to be cooked — and one with a tight-fitting lid. Prevent pottery lids from sticking by brushing edges with oil.
- Remove excess fat by a) allowing meat to cool and fat solidify — lift off fat with a spoon; b) brushing top of hot meat with a thick slice of bread — this will absorb the surface fat; c) placing ice-cubes on surface of casserole (fat clings to ice).
- A teaspoon or so of a dried herb or spice adds character to an ordinary meat dish for little extra cost — a worthwhile investment. Store in airtight containers.

Cuts of meat which may be casseroled
Budget cuts appear first in each list.

BEEF	VEAL	LAMB/MUTTON
shin	usually sold as stewing veal — similar to beef	boned forequarter (sold in piece)
gravy beef		flap
chuck		round neck chops
skirt		shoulder chops
thinflank		leg meat
thickflank		
blade		
topside		
	TRADITIONAL PORK	**TRIM PORK**
	belly pork	Y-bone steaks
	pork pieces	scotch fillet
	foreloin chops	diced pork
	foreloin and leg meat	mince
		leg steaks

SOUR CREAM VEAL

Serves 5-6
Fairly rich — serve with baked potatoes and baked tomatoes.

1 kg lean stewing veal	2 T flour
Salt, freshly ground black pepper	1 cup sour cream
2 T butter	220 g can sliced mushrooms in sauce
2 T oil	¼ t paprika
1 medium onion, finely chopped	

Cut veal into cubes. Sprinkle with salt and pepper. Heat butter and oil in heavy pan. Sauté meat in batches until browned on all sides. Turn into a casserole.

Sauté onion until soft and add to meat. Stir flour into frypan, add sour cream and mushrooms. Cook, stirring over low heat for 1-2 minutes. Season with paprika, salt and pepper. Pour over meat. Add a little hot water if too thick. Cover and cook 160°C for 1½ hours, or until meat is tender.

SOYA LAMB CHOPS

Serves 6
An economy casserole. The lamb is enhanced by a tasty combination of sauces and spices.

6 lamb shoulder or neck chops	3 T each tomato sauce, soy sauce and vinegar
2 T flour	2 T brown sugar
½ t salt	1 t curry powder
Pepper	1 apple, grated
2 T oil	1¼ cups stock
2 onions, sliced	Chopped parsley
1 clove garlic, crushed	

Remove any excess fat from chops. Toss in combined flour, salt and pepper. Brown quickly in hot oil and place in a shallow casserole.

Sauté onion and garlic. Add sauces, sugar and curry powder. Simmer gently for a few minutes and pour over meat. Add apple and stock. Cover and cook 180°C for 1½-2 hours. Thicken if necessary with a little cornflour mixed to a paste with water. Remove any surface fat and sprinkle with chopped parsley to serve.

LAMB AND PINEAPPLE

Serves about 6
Sweet and spicy, a casserole for family or guests. Choose meat from a boned forequarter of lamb, shoulder chops or from the leg.

1 kg boneless lean lamb	3 rashers bacon, diced
3 T flour	⅛ t cayenne pepper
2 T oil	Salt
340 g can pineapple pieces	1 t ground ginger
2 onions, sliced	¾ cup pineapple juice (or water)

Remove excess fat from lamb. Cut into 3 cm dice. Toss in flour — reserve excess flour. Heat oil and brown meat in batches. Place in a casserole. Drain pineapple and reserve syrup. Lightly brown pineapple pieces in frypan and add to meat. Lightly fry onions and bacon and add to casserole.

Stir reserved flour, seasonings, pineapple juice (or water) and reserved pineapple syrup into frypan. Scrape any burnt pieces from sides. Stir until boiling, then pour over ingredients in casserole.

Cover and cook 180°C for 1½-2 hours.

BEEF, BACON AND OYSTER CASSEROLE

Serves 5
Rather special.

700 g chuck or blade steak	3 T flour
2 rashers bacon	1 T oil
1 bayleaf	1 T butter
1 sprig parsley	1 cup red wine or stock
1 large onion, chopped	12 large oysters
1 large carrot, chopped	Small bacon rolls for garnish (optional)
100 g mushrooms, sliced	
Salt, freshly ground black pepper	

Cut meat into 3 cm cubes. Dice bacon. Combine meats with bayleaf, parsley, onion, carrot and mushrooms. Sprinkle with salt, pepper and flour — mix well.

Heat oil and butter in a wide pan — sauté mixture in batches until slightly browned. Turn into a casserole dish. Pour in wine. Cover and cook 160°C for 2 hours. Add oysters and any oyster liquid. Bake a further 30 minutes.

Garnish with small rolls of bacon which have been grilled. Serve with baked potatoes and a crisp salad.

ONE-POT BEEF DINNER

Serves 6-8
A fine example of how versatile a casserole can be; it economises on time, dishes and fuel too. This one will become a favourite — vegetables, beef and spices are cooked in one big pot.

- 2 T oil
- 2 medium onions, sliced
- 1 kg stewing beef
- 1 bayleaf
- ¼ t turmeric
- ½ t oregano
- 1 t ground cumin
- 2 cloves garlic, minced
- 2 t salt
- 5 whole black peppercorns
- 1 T vinegar
- 4 T tomato sauce
- 2 cups water
- 4 medium carrots, cut into sticks
- 3 medium potatoes, cut into sticks
- 2 stalks celery, cut into 5 cm pieces
- 1 cup frozen beans or peas
- 2 large cobs corn (fresh or frozen)

Heat oil in a large heavy casserole or frypan. Cook onion until transparent. Cut meat into 4 cm cubes and add to onions in casserole. Add seasonings, vinegar, sauce and water. Cover and cook 160°C for 1½ hours.

Add carrots, potatoes and celery to meat mixture, coating them well with casserole juices. Cover and cook a further 30 minutes. Add beans and corn, cut into 4 cm lengths. Thicken if desired with 3 T cornflour mixed to a paste with a little of the casserole liquid. Cover and return to oven for a further 30 minutes.

Serve straight from casserole, accompanied by crispy bread.

COUNTRY-STYLE PORK

Serves about 6
Easy to prepare.

- 1 kg lean pork
- 1 t salt
- 1½ T paprika
- 1 t ground ginger
- 1 T sugar
- 2 T flour
- 1 large onion, sliced
- 2 stalks celery, sliced
- Juice and rind of ½ lemon
- ¾ cup medium dry white wine
- 1 chicken stock cube
- ½ cup hot water
- Chopped parsley
- Sour cream

Cut pork into small cubes. Combine salt, paprika, ginger, sugar and flour in bowl. Toss meat in the dry ingredients, pressing mixture in well. Turn into a casserole. Add onion, celery, lemon rind and juice, wine and chicken stock cube dissolved in hot water.

Cover and bake 180°C for 2 hours. Serve on rice sprinkled with parsley and accompanied by sour cream.

PORK AND CRUNCHY VEGETABLE BAKE

Serves 3-4

Meat, vegetables and noodles are cooked in this slightly oriental dish.

500 g lean pork	3 stalks celery, diced
¼ cup flour	120 g fine noodles
Salt and pepper	220 g can mushroom soup
2 T oil	¼ cup milk
1 T finely chopped root ginger	1 cup fresh breadcrumbs
1 medium onion, diced	3 T melted butter
1 green pepper, sliced	1 clove garlic, crushed

Cut pork into small dice. Toss with flour, salt and pepper in paper bag. Heat oil in heavy frypan and brown meat on all sides. Add ginger, onion, green pepper and celery. Cover and let steam over low heat for about 10 minutes.

Meanwhile cook noodles in plenty of boiling water until just tender. Drain. Arrange in base of a greased casserole. Combine soup and milk, stir into meat mixture, then spoon contents of frypan over noodles in casserole.

Toss breadcrumbs in combined melted butter and garlic. Sprinkle over meat mixture. Bake uncovered 180°C for about 1 hour. The only accompaniment needed is hot, buttered bread.

ROASTING THE RIGHT WAY

The original meaning of roasting was 'to cook in front of, or over, a fierce glowing heat with the food rotating on a spit'. Today the term roasting is loosely used — 'baking' would be a far better description. Usually, less expensive cuts of meat are cooked whole, at moderate temperatures, for 25-30 minutes per 500 g. Tender cuts (such as the last 4 listed under BEEF below) can be roasted for shorter times at higher temperatures.

Lamb
The traditional leg of lamb is forever popular. But it need not always be roasted. For a smaller roast to serve 2-3 people, bone the leg and cut it in half crossways. Use the shank end half for roasting — stuff and tie with string. The other half of the leg may be cut into thin schnitzels, thicker steaks or cubed and threaded on skewers to be grilled.

Shank end legs
A leg of lamb, veal or pork may be cut in half crossways to produce 2 joints; the end with the long bone or shank is called the 'shank end leg'. The meatier portion is called the 'fillet' end.

Cuts of meat which may be roasted

BEEF
topside
bolar
rolled rib
prime rib
sirloin
rump
wing rib
cubed roll
fillet

VEAL
fillet (topside, thickflank or bolar)
loin

TRADITIONAL PORK
leg
loin
foreloin
rolled belly

LAMB/MUTTON
leg
loin
flap
ribs
forequarter
raised shoulder

TRIM PORK
shoulder
rolled roast
silverside
topside

Temperatures and times for roasting
A meat thermometer for roasting is used regularly by some cooks. Press the thermometer into the meatiest part of the joint, making sure it is not next to the bone as this will give a false reading. When the required temperature is reached, it will be indicated on the thermometer and the meat will be cooked.

MEAT	MINUTES/500 g at 180°C	INTERNAL TEMPERATURE	
Beef	10-15	60°C	rare (for tender cuts)
	15-20	70°C	medium
	25-30	75°C	well done
Veal	25-30	75°C	just done
Lamb	20-25	75°C	medium
	25-30	80°C	well done
Mutton	30	80°C	well done
Pork	35-40	85°C	well done

RARE RUMP ROAST

Serves 8-10

A very special roast. Suggested accompaniments: Yorkshire pudding (p.28), sautéed potatoes and salad.

2.5 kg corner piece of beef rump
Salt, freshly ground black pepper

2 cloves garlic, cut into slivers
4 T butter, melted
1½ cups red wine

Rub surface of meat with salt and pepper. With point of a sharp knife, make several slits in meat to insert garlic. Brush meat with melted butter. Place meat on rack in roasting pan lean side up, and roast at 250°C for 10 minutes. Turn meat fat side up and continue roasting at 180°C for a further 10 minutes per 500 g.

Remove meat to heated serving dish and keep warm in warming drawer for 10 minutes while making sauce. Drain off all except 1 T fat from roasting pan. Add wine and boil until reduced by one third. Serve with sliced meat.

GARLIC LEG OF LAMB

This leg is different! Cook a little longer if you prefer your lamb well done. Finely chopped root ginger may be substituted for garlic. Legs of lamb weigh between 1.25 and 2.5 kg.

- 1 leg of lamb
- ¼ cup dry breadcrumbs
- ¼ cup wholemeal flour
- 1 T sesame seeds
- 1 t salt
- 6 cloves garlic, sliced

Remove shank from leg, score and cross the leg (as you would a ham). Roll in combined breadcrumbs, flour, sesame seeds and salt. Place garlic along the cut lines of lamb.

Roast (with no added fat) at 180°C for 20-25 minutes per 500 g until just pink inside and crisp and brown outside. Serve with minted potatoes, buttered and nutmeg carrots, peas and gravy. (Make gravy in the usual way — see page 28.)

Garlic Leg of Lamb

SPICED ROLLED ROAST BEEF

Serves 6-8

The meat is marinated in a combination of spices and yoghurt, then roasted. Choose any rolled beef roast.

- 3 T lemon juice
- 1 t salt
- ½ t freshly ground black pepper
- ¼ t cayenne pepper
- 1.5-2 kg rolled roast beef
- 2 T boiling water
- 1 small onion, chopped
- ¼ cup plain yoghurt
- 3 cloves garlic, coarsely chopped
- 1 T finely chopped root ginger
- 1 T mustard seeds
- 1 t cumin
- 3 T butter, melted

Mix lemon juice, salt and pepper. Rub evenly over meat. Place in large bowl. Pierce meat in several places with thin skewer. Combine all remaining ingredients — place in an electric blender, or beat until well mixed. Rub this mixture over surface of meat in bowl. Cover and marinate overnight in refrigerator.

Place meat on rack in shallow roasting pan in oven 180°C for 30 minutes per 500 g. Baste occasionally.

ROSEMARY VEAL

Choose a piece of the loin or a whole loin with bone in or out. This is a tender cut but, as with all veal, it should be 'just' cooked; not too much or it will be too dry; not too little or it will be too chewy. Ask the butcher to 'chine' the backbone to make the meat easier to carve.

- Loin of veal
- 3 T oil
- Salt, freshly ground black pepper
- 3 sprigs rosemary
- 1-2 cups dry white wine

Brush veal with oil and sprinkle well with salt and pepper. Place in roasting pan and lay sprigs of rosemary across meat. Roast at 190°C for 25 minutes per 500 g. Brush occasionally with oil or pan juices.

Make a thin gravy by removing excess fat from pan, adding wine and boiling until reduced by half. Stir all burnt pieces in pan into sauce. Serve with baked potatoes and salad.

ROLLED SEASONED LAMB

Shoulder serves 4. Forequarter serves 8
A forequarter is a large cut which is very juicy and economical. The shoulder itself is from the forequarter and is usually smaller than a leg. Either cuts may be used in this recipe.

1 shoulder or forequarter of lamb
Salt, freshly ground black pepper
1 cup cooked rice
½ cup sultanas
2 T lemon juice
2 rashers bacon
1 egg

Basting Sauce
⅓ cup red wine
2 T brown sugar
1 t mustard
1 t salt
Pepper

Ask your butcher to bone the shoulder for you. Rub lamb with salt and plenty of black pepper. Combine rice, sultanas soaked in lemon juice, chopped bacon and egg. Place seasoning inside meat, roll up, and tie securely with string.

To make basting sauce, combine wine, sugar, mustard, salt and pepper and bring to the boil. Brush meat with this sauce. Roast 30 minutes per 500 g at 180°C, brushing occasionally with sauce.

Make gravy in usual way (see page 28). Serve with roasted kumara, a green vegetable and raw carrot sticks.

ROASTED PORK LOIN

Serves 6-7
These juicy cutlets are cooked in one piece and served with crackling (p. 28). Pork will be an even grey-white when cooked.

1 rib end of a loin of pork (6-7 cutlets)
3 T soft butter
1 t thyme

1 bayleaf
1 t dry mustard
Salt, freshly ground black pepper

Score rind of pork following direction of bones. Combine butter, thyme, crumbled bayleaf and mustard. Spread over rind, season with salt and pepper. Stand for about 2 hours before roasting.

Arrange meat, rind upwards, in roasting pan. Roast at 230°C for 15 minutes. Reduce heat to 180°C for 40 minutes per 500 g.

Make gravy in usual way (see page 28). Serve with mashed potatoes, red cabbage, baked apples or apple sauce.

ROAST ACCOMPANIMENTS

Beef: Yorkshire pudding, mustard, horseradish sauce, thin gravy or sauce
Veal: mustard, wine sauce
Lamb: mint sauce or jelly, redcurrant jelly, thick gravy
Pork: mustard, apple sauce, sage stuffing, crackling, medium gravy

YORKSHIRE PUDDING

1 cup flour
¼ t salt
1 egg

1¼ cups milk
1-2 T drippings from roast

Sift flour and salt into bowl. Make well in centre and add egg. Beat into flour, gradually adding half the milk. Beat constantly incorporating flour from sides of bowl. Beat well — stir in remaining milk. Refrigerate 30 minutes.

Place drippings in small baking dish and heat. When very hot add batter and bake in hot oven, 250°C until well browned, about 15-20 minutes. Individual puddings can be cooked in deep muffin tins.

PORK CRACKLING

For successful crackling, the skin of the pork should be scored before cooking. If skin has not been scored by the butcher, use the tip of a sharp knife and cut parallel lines just through the skin, at about 1.5 cm intervals. Brush skin with a little oil and rub with salt. Place meat in a hot oven, 230°C for 15 minutes. Reduce heat to 180°C until cooked. If crackling is still not crisp, lift off whole piece of scored skin and place back in hot oven by itself for 10-15 minutes. Replace on pork before serving.

GRAVY

Remove excess fat from roasting pan. Pour in 1-2 cups stock or wine; bring to boil on top of range, scraping any burnt pieces from pan into liquid. Season. Thicken if desired, with a little flour, cornflour or arrowroot mixed to a thick paste with water. Cook a few minutes and season to taste.

FRYING AND GRILLING THOSE TENDER CUTS

Frying and grilling are popular methods of cooking meat because they are quick. The rapid cooking produces a very good flavour — but it is suited only to the more tender cuts of meat. As there are just a few suitable cuts in most carcasses, it means that frying and grilling cuts are more expensive. However, when time is short, these are the cuts for you to try.

Cuts of meat which may be grilled or fried

BEEF
fillet
rump
sirloin
T-bone
scotch fillet
rib steak
crosscut
topside (stir fry)

VEAL
cutlets
schnitzels
chops
T-bone
(similar to beef)

TRADITIONAL PORK
leg chops/steaks
loin chops
rib chops
foreloin chops
pork fillets
schnitzels

LAMB
shoulder chops
rib cutlets
loin chops
leg steaks/chops
schnitzels

TRIM PORK
Y-bone steaks
medallions
butterfly steaks
mid-loin steaks
rump steaks
schnitzels
scotch fillet

Fat fires
If a fat fire starts on your range or in your frypan, turn off the source of heat at once. Cover flame with lid or throw salt, baking soda or sand onto the blaze, if a foam-type fire extinguisher is not at hand. *Never* try to put out a fat fire with water or flour. Water spreads the blaze and flour may explode.

A FAST GRILL

Grilling (known by Americans as broiling) is a quick method of cooking by radiant heat supplied by electricity, gas or charcoal.

Hints
- Lean meats are best brushed with butter or oil during cooking to prevent drying out.
- The grill should be preheated 10-15 minutes on high. The heat may be reduced if necessary after initial cooking.
- The grill rack should be rubbed with fat or oil before food is placed on it.
- The cooking time will vary with the thickness of the meat.
- Turn the meat with tongs or spoons to avoid tearing the surface and losing any juices.

VEAL CUTLETS STUFFED WITH BACON

Serves 4

Cutlets are boneless and are cut from the loin. A few chopped mushrooms may be added to the stuffing too.

- 4 thick veal cutlets
- 1 medium onion, finely diced
- 2 rashers bacon, finely diced
- 1 T butter
- Freshly ground black pepper
- Melted butter

With a sharp knife, slice from one edge nearly to the other through the middle of the cutlet to form a pocket.

Sauté onions and bacon in butter until onions are transparent and bacon cooked. Cool, season with pepper and stuff into cutlets. Secure edges with toothpicks and brush with melted butter.

Preheat grill 10 minutes. Place cutlets under grill and cook 5-6 minutes each side, brushing with melted butter occasionally. Do not overcook (the cutlets should be lightly browned). Remove toothpicks and serve with warmed sour cream as sauce.

POHUTUKAWA LAMB KEBABS

Serves 3-4
Use lamb from shoulder or leg.

500 g lean lamb, cubed
2 t sugar
1 T sherry
1 T tomato sauce
1 T vinegar
2 T soy sauce
1 t curry powder
1 T oil

Place cubed lamb in bowl. Combine all remaining ingredients and pour over lamb. Turn meat to make sure it is well coated. Allow to stand for at least 2 hours.
　Thread meat on skewers and cook under preheated grill, 10 minutes each side. Vegetables such as small tomatoes, courgettes, green peppers, and small whole onions can be skewered and grilled alongside the meat kebabs. Brush with melted butter during cooking.

Pohutukawa Lamb Kebabs

HONEYED PORK FINGERS

Serves 3-4
Pork fingers or slices are cut from the belly. If possible, choose long fingers for this recipe.

6-8 long pork fingers (approx. 2 per adult)	1 T soy sauce
2 T honey	2 T water
	1 T tomato sauce

Slit fat down fingers at 3 cm intervals. Combine remaining ingredients, mix well. Marinate fingers for 2-3 hours at room temperature.
    Preheat grill. Remove fingers, twist, and place on grilling rack. Grill about 8 cm beneath source of heat, for 8-10 minutes each side.

PEPPERED RUMP STEAK

Serves 4
A more economical beef grill that a fillet, sirloin or T-bone.

| 1 rump steak 4 cm thick, weighing 500-600 g | Melted butter |
| Freshly ground black pepper | Salt |

The steak should be at room temperature before cooking. Slit fat in 2-3 places around side to prevent curling. Sprinkle both sides of steak with generous amount of pepper, press pepper in well and brush with melted butter.
    Preheat grill 10 minutes. Place steak under grill for 8-10 minutes each side until well browned. Place on hot serving dish. Cut across steak in 3 cm slices and sprinkle with salt. Serve immediately.
    Delicious with horseradish sauce: combine 2 t grated horseradish with ½ cup sour cream.

Peppered Rump Steak

THE ART OF PAN FRYING

With very little effort, tender cuts of meat can be transformed into the exotic — with the aid of a good quality frypan or skillet and an eye on the clock.

Choose a heavy-based frypan with just enough fat, butter or oil to prevent the food sticking to it. It is important not to overcook these juicy cuts.

Oriental stir fry cookery is a type of pan frying.

PERFECT PAN-FRIED STEAKS

Choose steaks no less than 1 cm thick, but preferably 3 cm or more. Steaks suitable for pan frying include:

- **Fillet:** only 2 per animal so expensive. The whole fillet is known as 'tenderloin'. Steak cut from the thick end of the fillet is called 'undercut', and steak from the middle is called the 'eye'.
- **Sirloin:** also called porterhouse.
- **T-bone:** identified by large T-bone. Good flavour.
- **Scotch fillet:** well marbled. Cut from ribs and sometimes called 'cubed roll'. Not commonly seen as it is usually included in prime rib roasts.
- **Entrecôte:** also called 'rib' steaks. Other part of prime rib roast so not often seen.
- **Rump steak, crosscut blade, oyster blade:** all best marinated before cooking, not as tender as preceding cuts. All more economical and have a coarser texture.

To cook steak:
Wipe the steak and cut through any fat and connective tissue on outer edge of meat, to prevent curling during cooking.

Preheat heavy frypan (an electric frypan is quite suitable). Melt 1-2 T fat, oil or butter or a mixture of butter and oil — this gives a good flavour. Heat until very hot, swirling it around pan. Place meat in pan, turn heat to medium/high. Turn occasionally.

Cook steaks 3 cm thick 4-5 minutes each side for rare steak, 5-6 minutes each side for medium steak. Steak should not be overcooked as it dries out quickly. Season if desired.

PAPER-THIN PEPPER STEAKS

Serves 4

Choose boneless topside or rump steak cut no more than 5 mm thick. An economical pan fry.

4 large topside schnitzels	1 small onion, finely chopped
Freshly ground black pepper	½ t salt
2 T butter	½ cup red wine
2 T oil	Chopped parsley

Sprinkle both sides of schnitzels generously with pepper. Heat butter and oil in heavy frypan. Brown meat quickly over high heat. Place on hot platter. Sauté onion in pan with salt. Add wine. Bring to the boil. Dip each steak into liquid for about 15 seconds. Place on serving dish. Boil liquid and pour over steaks. Sprinkle with parsley.

LAMB NOISETTES

Serves 6-8

Ask your butcher to bone and roll a loin or middle loin of lamb. This can be cut into steaks and pan fried, or roasted whole and then sliced. It is a most attractive cut of lamb.

1.25 kg boned and rolled loin of lamb, tied with string every 4 cm	Oil
	⅓ cup brandy
Salt and pepper	⅔ cup cream
4 cloves garlic	½ cup redcurrants (in season or use jelly)
1-2 T dried tarragon	

Rub lamb with salt and pepper. Crush garlic and pound with tarragon. Spread lamb with this mixture and pan fry or roast.

To pan fry, cut steaks in middle between each string, leaving 1 string per steak. Heat 2 T oil in heavy frypan and fry noisettes on medium heat, 10 minutes each side. Transfer to hot platter and keep warm.

To roast, place in roasting dish and brush with a little oil. Roast 180°C for about 45 minutes. Place lamb on warm platter and cut into noisettes.

Retain pan juices, add brandy and cream. Bring to boil and simmer for a few minutes, stirring constantly. Add redcurrants or jelly, heat through and pour over noisettes.

VEAL WITH CREAM SAUCE

Serves 4

The sauce is great with veal T-bone, cutlet, chop, veal rump or even schnitzel. It is important not to overcook veal.

4 veal T-bones or 600–700 g boneless veal frying steak	1 clove garlic, crushed
Freshly ground black pepper	Salt and pepper
2 T flour	1 t paprika
2 T butter	½ cup red wine
2 T oil (preferably olive)	2 T tomato sauce
1 small onion, minced	1 t sugar
	½ cup cream or sour cream

Season meat with pepper and sprinkle with flour. In heavy frypan, heat butter and oil. Pan fry meat over medium-high heat for 4–5 minutes each side (schnitzels 2 minutes each side). Cover for 2 minutes of cooking time. Transfer to heated platter and keep warm.

Pan fry onion and garlic until soft. Season with salt, pepper and paprika. Pour in wine, sauce and sugar. Boil 1 minute, stirring. Lastly add cream; bring to boiling point and pour over meat. Serve with sautéed potatoes and a green vegetable.

PORK SCHNITZEL WITH FRUITY SAUCE

Serves 4

A pork schnitzel is a thin, boneless slice of pork cut from either a boned shoulder of pork, from the rib end of the loin, or sometimes from a boned leg. Veal schnitzels may also be used.

4 pork schnitzels	**Fruity Sauce**
Flour	¼ cup apricot purée
Salt and pepper	¼ cup tomato sauce
1 egg, beaten	½ t curry powder
½–¾ cup dry breadcrumbs	¼ t ground ginger
2 T butter	1 t cornflour
2 T oil	

Snip rind or fat around meat to prevent curling during cooking. Pound meat gently if schnitzel is too thick. Dip into flour which has been seasoned with salt and pepper — press in well. Dip into egg, then into breadcrumbs. Press in well. Melt butter and oil in frypan and sauté schnitzels over medium heat for about 3 minutes each side. Serve 'as is' or with fruity sauce.

To make sauce, combine apricot purée (sieved cooked apricots), tomato sauce, curry powder, ginger and cornflour. Bring slowly to boil, and cook, stirring, for 2 minutes.

Veal with Cream Sauce

LAMB STEAKS WITH CAPERS AND CHEESE

Serves 4
Lamb steaks can be cut from a boned leg of lamb.

4 lamb steaks 3 cm thick	1 T butter
4 slices tasty cheese	1 T oil
4 t capers	Salt
Freshly ground black pepper	**Chopped parsley**

Make pocket in side of each steak, large enough to insert a slice of cheese and 1 t capers. Secure with toothpicks, season with pepper.

In heavy pan, heat butter and oil. Pan fry steaks on medium-high heat, 5-6 minutes each side. Sprinkle with salt and parsley and serve with minted potatoes and peas.

FRYING TIME

By plunging food into a large quantity of hot oil or fat, it can be cooked to crusty perfection on the outside, while remaining juicy and full of flavour inside.

For shallow frying, oil, 1.5-2 cm deep, is heated in a heavy frypan. This is suitable for cuts of meat such as cutlets which have been coated in egg and breadcrumbs. Turn midway during cooking.

In deep frying, enough oil is heated to fully immerse the food to be fried. Generally, oil to a minimum depth of 5-8 cm is required. Use a heavy saucepan about 15 cm deep. Fondues are an example of deep frying.

The correct oil temperature is important. If the oil or fat is too cold, it soaks into the food. Try frying a little at a time so as not to lower the oil temperature. About 190°C is the temperature at which to fry meats. If you do not have a thermometer, wait until a faint haze rises from the oil, then drop in a cube of bread. If the bread browns on one side in about 20 seconds, the temperature is right for frying. After it is cooked, briefly drain food on absorbent paper.

BEEF RIBBONS

Appetiser serves 8. Buffet serves 4-6
Serve as an appetiser or as part of a buffet meal. Store drained marinade in refrigerator and use in casseroles or soups.

500 g rump steak
¼ cup oil
¼ cup red wine
2 T tomato sauce
1 T golden syrup

2 cloves garlic, crushed
½ t curry powder
Oil for frying
Chopped parsley
Sesame seeds

Cut beef into very thin strips, about 8 × 3 cm. Combine oil, wine, sauce, syrup, garlic and curry powder, and pour over meat. Marinate for 2 hours at room temperature.

Drain and pat dry. Thread on small skewers in ribbon or accordion style. Heat 5 cm oil in saucepan to 200°C. Cook skewered meat in hot oil for 1-2 minutes until brown on outside but still juicy inside. Serve on or off skewers, garnished with chopped parsley and sesame seeds.

LEMON CRUMBED CUTLETS

Serves 4

Cutlets are taken from the rib end of a loin of lamb. Lamb cutlets are long and slender — the ends can be decorated with paper frills.

- 8 lamb cutlets (2 per person)
- ¼ cup flour
- 1 egg
- ¼ cup milk
- 1 cup dry breadcrumbs
- Grated rind of 1 lemon
- ½ t marjoram
- 2 T parsley, finely chopped
- Oil for frying

Dip cutlets in flour, then in lightly beaten egg and milk. Combine breadcrumbs, lemon rind, marjoram and parsley and press crumb mixture firmly onto cutlets. Refrigerate for 30 minutes to allow crumb coating to set.

Heat about 2 cm oil in wide frypan. Fry cutlets until cooked and golden brown, about 5 minutes each side. Serve with lemon wedges.

Lemon Crumbed Cutlets

VEAL CHOW MEIN

Serves 4
An attractive one-pan dinner.

400 g lean frying veal	1 red pepper (optional)
4 T oil	1½ cups chicken stock
1 large onion	1 T soy sauce
1 large carrot	1 t raw sugar
50 g mushrooms	2 t arrowroot
4 cups chopped cabbage (preferably Chinese cabbage)	Crispy noodles

Slice veal into long strips, 5 mm wide. Heat 2 T oil in wok or frypan and quickly fry meat in batches until brown. Remove and keep warm.

Slice vegetables thinly. Heat remaining oil and stir fry onions until transparent. Add carrots and cook a further minute. Add mushrooms, cabbage and pepper — stir another minute. Pour in stock, soy sauce and sugar and bring to boil.

Mix arrowroot with a little water and stir into pan. Add veal and reheat gently until thickened and heated through. Serve with crispy noodles.

To prepare crispy noodles, boil egg noodles until just tender. Drain and cool. Deep fry in batches until crisp. Store in an airtight container.

BEEF AND TOMATOES

Serves 4
This meat needs to be sliced paper thin. Cut while half frozen if possible.

500 g thickflank or blade	1 small onion, finely chopped
1 clove garlic, chopped	1 t sugar
1 t finely chopped root ginger	½ t vinegar
2 T oil	1 t soy sauce
500 g tomatoes, quartered	

Slice meat thinly. Place garlic and ginger in frypan with oil. Heat and cook until garlic has dried out. Discard garlic and ginger. Quickly fry steak until just cooked and remove from pan.

Cook tomatoes, onion, sugar, vinegar and soy sauce in pan, stirring until mixture boils. Add steak and stir fry until heated through. Serve on rice.

Veal Chow Mein

STIR FRIED RICE AND PORK

Serves 3-4

Cook the rice the day before to allow it to become dry enough for pan frying.

400 g lean pork	Oil
1 T dry sherry	2 eggs, lightly beaten
1 T soy sauce	4 cups cooked long grain rice
1 T cornflour	½ cup toasted cashew nuts
1 t sugar	1 spring onion, finely chopped

Cut pork into thin shreds. Mix sherry, soy sauce, cornflour and sugar and toss pork in this mixture until well coated. Heat 2 T oil in frypan and stir fry pork until cooked, about 2-3 minutes. Set aside. Wipe pan clean. Pour in 1 T oil. Heat, then add eggs. Gently push eggs back and forth in pan until set. Transfer cooked omelette immediately to bowl and break or cut up.

Pour 2 T oil in pan and add rice. Stir fry for 2 minutes until all grains are coated with oil. Add pork, nuts, egg and spring onion and cook long enough to heat through. Serve immediately with soy sauce.

Stir Fried Rice and Pork

FUN FONDUES

Not only are they fun, but eating the fondue way is very relaxed, requiring little preparation time and allowing everyone to cook their own.

With oil or 'bourguinonne' fondues, cubes of tender meat are deep fried at the table, in a communal pot. A long-handled fork, an eating fork and a plate should be provided for each diner. A fondue pot containing hot oil is placed in the centre of the table.

Choose a 1-litre pot with steep sides to prevent splattering. A spirit burner keeps the oil at cooking temperature 190°C. An electric saucepan could be used as a substitute.

Fondues should be accompanied by 3 or more sauces into which the cooked meat is dipped. Serve with a crisp salad, hot buttered bread, and perhaps gherkins and pickled onions.

MIXED MEAT FONDUE

Choose a selection of boneless, lean, tender meat, such as sirloin steak, frying veal, lamb steak and pork. Or, if preferred, just one type of meat may be used.

225 g meat per person **1¼ cups salad oil**
100 g butter

Cut meat into cubes of about 3 cm and layer attractively on a plate. Heat butter and oil in fondue pot on stove. When mixture is bubbling, transfer pot to the spirit burner and regulate heat so it retains cooking temperature.

Each person selects a mixture of meats to put on their dinner plate. They then spear one piece of meat at a time with fondue fork and place into hot oil for a minute, or until cooked according to taste. The meat is then removed to the dinner plate. With eating fork, meat is dipped into one of the sauces (such as those on p. 46) and eaten.

LAMB AND CHEESE BALL FONDUE

Serves 3-4
A rather different fondue and a little more economical. Prepare meatballs in advance and refrigerate.

500 g minced lamb	1 egg, beaten
2 T dry breadcrumbs	150 g soft cheese (Colby)
1 T minced onion	1½ cups salad oil
½ t curry powder	

Combine lamb, breadcrumbs, onion, curry powder and egg. Cut cheese into small cubes of about 1 cm. Shape enough meat around each piece of cheese to form a 3 cm meatball. Roll gently in hands.

Pour oil into fondue pot to depth of 5 cm, but no more than half full, and heat to 190°C, or until a cube of bread browns in about 20 seconds.

Serve meatballs at room temperature on a serving platter, spear balls with fondue fork and fry in hot oil for about 2 minutes, or until browned. Transfer to dinner plate, dip in sauce and eat. Serve with a selection of sauces and pickles.

SAUCES

A selection of commercially prepared sauces, pickles and chutneys can be served with the fondue, such as plum sauce, tomato relish and apple chutney. Or you can make your own, using the following recipes.

HORSERADISH CREAM WHIP

2 hard-boiled eggs	Salt
1 t prepared mustard	½ cup cream
1-2 T prepared horseradish	

Mash eggs well and blend with mustard, horseradish and salt. Whip cream until just stiff. Fold in egg mixture. Makes about 1 cup.

MUSTARD SAUCE

2 T prepared mustard	¾ cup mayonnaise
1 T lemon juice	

Mix all ingredients together and refrigerate for several hours before serving. Makes ¾ cup, enough for 6-8.

ONION SAUCE

¾ cup sour cream
½ packet onion soup mix
2 spring onions, chopped

Combine ingredients and refrigerate for several hours before serving. Makes about 1 cup.

BASIL BUTTER

150 g butter
1-2 t dried basil
1 T lemon juice

Cream softened butter until light and fluffy. Beat in basil and lemon juice. Stand at room temperature for 1 hour before serving. Makes about ¾ cup. This is especially good with pork.

BARBECUES FOR OUTDOOR LIVING

Barbecues appeal to all ages and groups, and although children may prefer their meat 'plain', there are infinite ways to dress up meat for adults.

A good fire is essential. Charcoal is the most popular barbecue fuel, although briquets give a more prolonged heat and are a better fuel for cooking larger cuts of meat. To light the fire, soak a few pieces of charcoal in a tin with a little methylated spirits for about 10 minutes. Place on the barbecue with some more charcoal. Stand back, and place a match near a piece of treated charcoal. Firelighters may also be used — place under a cone of charcoal or briquets and light.

Whatever method you choose, allow about 30 minutes between lighting up and cooking. The charcoal should be ash-grey by day and have a red glow by night — no flames. Gas-fired barbecues provide instant heat.

SOY AND GINGER STEAK

Serves 6

This marinade has universal appeal. It may be made in bulk and stored in the refrigerator. Good on most meats and has a tenderising effect.

6 steaks, (rump or sirloin) weighing about 170 g and cut about 3 cm thick
½ cup soy sauce
2 T firmly packed brown sugar
¼ cup sherry
1 clove garlic, crushed
2 t finely grated root ginger
2 T salad oil

Trim steaks and place in single layer in flat pan. Combine soy sauce, sugar, sherry, garlic, ginger and salad oil. Mix well and pour over steaks. Marinate meat up to 8 hours, turning occasionally. Drain excess marinade from steaks. Place meat on grill over hot coals. Grill about 5 minutes each side.

OUTDOOR PORK

Serves 6

This marinade suits all cuts of pork.

6 pork chops or steaks (preferably cut from the forequarter)
¼ cup dry sherry
½ cup tomato purée
1 t ground ginger
1 small onion, grated
1 t mustard
2 T honey
1 T Worcestershire sauce
2 T oil

Snip rind of chops and place in single layer in a flat pan. Combine all other ingredients well. Pour over pork and marinate for at least 4 hours. Drain excess marinade from meat and barbecue over hot coals for about 12-15 minutes each side, or until cooked as desired.

Barbecue Assortment

PIHA LAMB

Serves 4-6

Lamb is excellent on the barbecue. Try lamb steaks or chops either left whole or cut into cubes and threaded on skewers. Marinate first in this mixture of onion, garlic and cumin.

1 kg lean lamb or lamb steaks
½ cup oil
¼ cup soy sauce
2 medium onions, grated

2 cloves garlic, crushed
1 T lemon juice
½ t cumin
2 T sesame seeds

Remove excess fat from meat. Cut into 3 cm cubes if lamb is to be skewered. Combine all other ingredients in bowl. Place meat in marinade for 1 hour or longer. Grill over hot coals, turning occasionally, for about 10-15 minutes.

MIXED KEBAB PLATTER

Serves 6

Skewer cookery is versatile and lends itself to do-it-yourself parties. Present a large tray of foods from which guests can choose and cook their own combinations. As some foods cook more slowly than others (small whole onions or new potatoes, for example), precook these before setting out. Corn can be cut into 3 cm rounds.

2 sirloin or scotch fillet steaks, cut in 3 cm cubes
1 pork fillet, sliced in 1 cm rounds
6 frankfurters, sliced diagonally
6 precooked sausages, cut into thirds
Cheerios or cocktail sausages

Meatballs (see method)
12 small tomatoes
2 green peppers, sliced
12 mushrooms
3 corn cobs, sliced
12 small whole onions, precooked

Take a selection of the above foods and lay attractively on a tray. Cover and refrigerate until ready to skewer.

To make meatballs, combine 500 g minced topside with 1 t oregano and 2 T milk powder and form into 3 cm balls.

When barbecue is ready, take a combination of meats and vegetables and thread on long skewers. Brush with oil and barbecue over glowing coals. Brush with oil during cooking if necessary. Turn often. When cooked, after about 5 minutes each side, remove food from skewers with a fork.

MARINATED SKEWERED VEAL

Serves 4-5

Veal cubes may be threaded alternately with halved pineapple slices if desired.

500 g frying veal
⅓ cup soy sauce
1 small onion, grated

1 T oregano
½ cup red wine
2 T salad oil

Cut veal into 4 cm cubes. Place in a bowl. Mix all other ingredients and pour over meat. Marinate 4-6 hours, turning often. About 1 hour before barbecuing, string meat on 4-5 skewers. Grill over hot coals about 15-20 minutes, turning about 4 times. Baste occasionally.

BARBECUED LUNCHEON

Serves 6-8

Especially popular with the younger set. Use whole 900 g luncheons or bologna. Smaller chubs will need a shorter cooking time.

900 g luncheon or bologna roll
50 g butter, melted

4 T brown sugar
1 t prepared mustard
Cloves

Remove casing, score surface by making cuts 3 cm apart and 5 mm deep. Brush with combined butter, brown sugar and mustard. Stud with cloves.

Skewer meat and grill at a little distance from coals, turning often. Baste. Meat may be cut thickly and sandwiched between a hamburger bun with onions, lettuce and sauce.

ACCOMPANIMENTS

- **Vegetables in foil:** these may be cooked in the coals. Potatoes take about 20 minutes, also try yams, corn, and onions. Wrap well in tin foil with a little added butter.
- **Blue cheese butter:** for plain steaks. Combine ½ cup blue cheese creamed with ¼ cup butter, 1 clove garlic (crushed), and 2 T minced parsley. Spoon onto cooked steaks.
- **Spinach salad:** crumble crisp cooked bacon and chopped spring onions into a bowl of washed, crisp, torn spinach. Toss with strong garlic French dressing.
- **Melon and cucumber salad:** mix cubes of watermelon and cucumber with lots of freshly cut mint just before serving.

PRESSURE COOKING

Cooking with a pressure cooker economises on time and fuel. Colourful, nutritious meals can be prepared in a quarter to a third of the usual time. Because of the wide range of cookers on the market, it is wise to follow the manufacturer's instructions carefully.

Hints
- Always make sure that the vent holes are clear.
- Never fill the cooker more than two-thirds full and only half full when making soups.
- Time the cooking from when the pressure registers.
- Food will continue to cook until pressure is released.

POTPOURRI

Serves about 6

A mixture of beef and vegetables — it can be a soup or a stew. Serve with hot rolls.

½ cup dried red kidney beans
2 T oil
2 cloves garlic, chopped
1 kg shin of beef on bone
1 large onion, chopped
6 peppercorns
1 t salt
1 t thyme
8 cups water
3 stalks celery, sliced
2 carrots, chopped
4 tomatoes or 2 T tomato paste
1 leek, sliced
2 potatoes, cubed
50 g fine spaghetti
Salt and pepper to taste
Tasty cheese, finely grated
Parsley

Wash beans and soak in water while preparing meat. Heat oil in pressure cooker (without lid). Sauté meat until slightly browned. Add garlic, onion, peppercorns, salt, thyme, water and beans. (Do not fill more than half full.) Place lid on pressure cooker. Cook under pressure for 25 minutes, according to manufacturer's instructions.

Remove meat from bones and dice. Remove surface fat from stock. Return meat to cooker. Add all remaining ingredients except cheese and parsley. Cook under pressure 10 minutes. Serve sprinkled with cheese and parsley.

SAVOURY LAMB CHOPS

Serves 4

A very tasty stew using round neck chops. Serve accompanied by a crisp salad and French bread.

- 6-8 lamb neck chops
- ½ cup red wine
- 1 onion, chopped
- 1 clove garlic, crushed
- 310 g can tomato soup
- 1 T prepared mustard
- 1 T each Worcestershire sauce, lemon juice and brown sugar

Arrange chops on base of the pressure cooker and pour red wine over. Cover and cook 20 minutes under pressure, according to manufacturer's instructions. Reduce pressure and pour off any excess fat.

Place all remaining ingredients into saucepan and bring to the boil. Pour over chops, replace lid of cooker, and cook under pressure 15 minutes.

Potpourri

DILL POT ROAST

Serves 6-8
A complete meal cooked in the pressure cooker.

1.5 kg rolled veal pot roast or fillet of veal	6 medium potatoes
2 T oil	1 t salt
1 large onion, chopped	Freshly ground black pepper
1 leek, sliced (or celery)	3 T flour
2 large carrots, chopped	3 T cold water
1 cup hot water	½ cup sour cream
½ t dill	

Brown veal on all sides in oil in pressure cooker (without lid). Remove to one side. Sauté chopped onion, leek and carrots for 2-3 minutes. Place veal on top of vegetables. Add hot water and ¼ t dill. Place lid on pressure cooker and cook 45 minutes, according to manufacturer's instructions.

Peel and halve potatoes. Place in pressure cooker with meat. Sprinkle with salt and pepper. Cook under pressure a further 10 minutes. Remove meat and vegetables to a hot platter.

Mix flour and water to a smooth paste. Stir into liquid in pressure cooker. Stir over low heat until thickened. Add remaining dill and sour cream. Serve chopped vegetables and potatoes with sliced veal and sour cream sauce.

GARLIC PORK CHOPS

Serves 4
Instant pork chops — use loin or foreloin.

4 pork chops	2 large cloves garlic
2 T butter	Thyme
2 T oil	Salt, freshly ground black pepper
4 large kumaras or potatoes	

Sauté chops on both sides until browned in melted butter and oil, in pressure cooker (without lid). Remove to one side.

Peel and halve kumaras. Place on base of cooker. Slice garlic cloves in quarters and place a quarter on each kumara together with a small sprig of thyme. Lay chops on top of kumaras and season with salt and pepper. Close lid and cook 15 minutes, according to manufacturer's instructions.

VARIETY MEATS

Many of the world's best restaurants serve liver and brains — they are not just 'poor man's' fare. The so-called 'variety meats' (offal) are a rich source of vitamins and minerals, at a low price. White offals, such as brains and sweetbreads, are easily digested and are therefore suitable for convalescent diets.

BRAINS

Calf, lamb, pork and beef brains can be poached, or shallow or deep fried. Lamb brains are the most popular and are often sold in pairs.

Soak brains in cold water for several hours. Place in saucepan with 1 D vinegar, a pinch of salt, 1 bayleaf and water to cover. Bring slowly to boiling point. Poach gently 10 minutes.

Drain and cover with cold water to firm. Remove membranes.

To serve, slice and heat in parsley sauce, pan fry in butter, or dip in egg and breadcrumbs and fry.

BRAIN SAVOURY

Serves 4

500 g lamb brains
4 T butter
1 small onion, chopped
4 T flour
¾ cup boiling water
1 chicken stock cube or similar
1 cup milk
1 T capers
4 stuffed olives, sliced
1 large tomato, skinned and chopped
½ green pepper, diced
Juice of ½ lemon

Prepare brains as directed. Cut into 3 cm cubes. Melt butter in heavy saucepan. Sauté onion until transparent, not brown. Stir in flour. Dissolve chicken stock cube in boiling water and allow to cool. Gradually add to saucepan with milk. Stir and cook until sauce thickens.

Add brains, capers, olives, tomato, green pepper and lemon juice. Simmer for 10 minutes. Serve as an entrée or main course, in a casserole or in vol-au-vent (pastry) cases.

SWEETBREADS

Animals possess two types of sweetbreads, one found in the throat and the other near the pancreas. The latter are the best. Sweetbreads are glands. Usually only calf and lamb sweetbreads are used in cooking.

Wash sweetbreads well. Soak in cold water for 4 hours, changing water every hour. Drain, place in saucepan with sufficient cold water to cover. Bring water slowly to the boil and simmer about 4 minutes.

Remove as much skin and membrane as possible. Dry well. Press a plate on top of sweetbreads, so they flatten as they cool. Serve warmed in a cream sauce or crumb and fry.

SWEETBREADS WITH MUSHROOMS

Serves 4-6

- 500 g lamb sweetbreads
- 2 T butter
- 170 g mushrooms
- 4 T flour
- ½ cup milk
- ¾ cup boiling water
- 1 chicken stock cube
- Salt, freshly ground black pepper
- 4 T cream

Prepare sweetbreads as directed but do not press. Chop roughly.

Melt butter in frypan. Sauté sliced mushrooms and sweetbreads for 2 minutes. Stir in flour and cook ½ minute. Add milk, boiling water with chicken stock cube dissolved in it, salt and pepper. Slowly bring to the boil, stirring. Simmer about 15 minutes. Stir in cream.

Serve as an entrée or luncheon dish, with or without a pastry or bread case.

TRIPE

Tripe is not often high on the popularity poll, but the following recipe is a winner with tripe lovers. Tripe can be boiled, casseroled or braised. It is prepared from the first and second part of an ox or sheep stomach.

Although it is purchased already blanched, it is best to cook it again in boiling water for 5 minutes, before using. Try to purchase fresh tripe and cook on the same day.

TRIPE WITH BACON AND TOMATOES

Serves 4

- 700 g tripe
- 2 onions, chopped
- 2 T butter
- 2 rashers bacon, chopped
- 2 cloves garlic, crushed
- 3 medium tomatoes, peeled and chopped
- 1 T tomato paste
- 1½ cups boiling water
- 2 chicken stock cubes
- Thyme and rosemary sprigs
- Salt, freshly ground black pepper
- Chopped parsley

Cut prepared tripe into strips. In heavy saucepan, sauté onions in butter until golden. Push to one side. Sauté bacon until cooked.

Add garlic, tomatoes, tomato paste, boiling water in which chicken stock cubes have been dissolved, thyme, rosemary, salt and pepper. Bring to the boil. Add tripe and reduce heat. Cover and simmer slowly 1-1½ hours. Transfer to serving dish and sprinkle with parsley.

Tripe with Bacon and Tomatoes

HEARTS

Ox, lamb and calf hearts can be sliced or left whole and can be braised, casseroled or roasted.

Soak in salted water for 1 hour. Remove tubes, gristle and excess fat. Hearts can then be stuffed, tied with string and braised or roasted whole, or sliced and used in stews. They need long slow cooking.

KIDNEYS

Ox, lamb, calf and pork kidneys can be fried, stewed or grilled. Ox kidney is large and usually only small amounts are purchased at one time. It is strongly flavoured and tougher than lamb or calf kidney. Pork kidney also has a strong odour.

Remove skin and fat. Cut through the centre lengthwise. Remove tubes. Pan fry or grill whole, or slice and use in combination with other meats.

MOCK STEAK AND KIDNEY PIE

Serves 4

3 lamb hearts
2 lamb kidneys
1 medium onion, chopped
1 medium carrot, chopped
½ t mixed herbs
¼ t nutmeg

Salt and pepper
1¼ cups stock
3 T flour
350 g flaky pastry
Milk

Prepare hearts and kidneys as directed. Cut into small pieces. Place in casserole or suitable pie dish with onion, carrot, mixed herbs, nutmeg, salt, pepper and stock. Sprinkle with flour. Mix well. Cover and cook 1½ hours at 160°C, stirring occasionally.

Roll out pastry on lightly floured board, 3 cm larger than top of casserole or pie dish. Cut 1 cm wide strip, place on edge of dish previously brushed with water.

Brush strip of pastry with milk, lift remaining pastry on, easing it gently. Press edges together and decorate with knife. (Use pie funnel in centre of the dish if necessary.) Glaze pastry with milk. Decorate with pastry scraps if desired. Cut vent in centre of pastry with sharp knife. Bake 190°C for 25 minutes or until cooked.

LIVER

Beef, calf, pork or lamb liver can be grilled, fried or braised. Lamb and calf liver, usually referred to as 'fry', is milder in flavour than pork or beef liver. Remove the fine skin if possible, and the gristle and tubes. Cut into slices for cooking.

HERBED LIVER PATE

¾ cup hot water
2 t powdered chicken stock
1½ t gelatine
2 T cold water
400 g lamb's fry, finely sliced
3 rashers bacon, chopped
75 g butter
1 clove garlic

¼ t oregano
¼ t thyme
1 bayleaf
2 T chopped parsley
1 t tomato paste
3 T sherry
¼ cup cream
Salt and pepper

Place hot water and stock into saucepan. Sprinkle gelatine over cold water, add to saucepan. Stir until combined. Bring to boil, remove from heat and allow to cool. Pour into base of an oiled 3-cup mould. Refrigerate until set.

Melt a third of the butter in large frypan. Cook liver, bacon, garlic and herbs for 15 minutes over low heat. Mince twice or place in blender with remaining ingredients including butter, melted. Mix well and season.

Spoon on top of set gelatine mixture. Press down gently. Refrigerate for at least 8 hours before serving. Unmould and serve with crackers or Melba toast.

TONGUE

Calf or ox tongues weigh about 1 kg. They are suitable for pressing and serving cold with salads, or serving hot with sauces. Lamb tongues are much smaller — buy 4 in place of 1 calf tongue.

1 calf or ox tongue
Water
1 onion

1 bayleaf
4 peppercorns
Sprig of thyme

Soak tongue for 4 hours in cold water. Drain. Place in large saucepan and cover with fresh water. Add remaining ingredients. Bring to boil slowly and simmer 2½ hours or until tender. Cool tongue in cold water for a few minutes, then skin and remove any fat, bones or gristle.

PRESSED TONGUE

Serves 6-8

Place in basin or mould just large enough to hold tongue when coiled. Add sufficient stock to fill the gaps. Place a flat plate on top. Put a weight on plate to press tongue down. Refrigerate until set. Unmould.

TONGUE WITH SPICY ORANGE SAUCE

Juice of 2 large oranges
1 T finely grated orange rind
1 cup water
1 T brown sugar
1 T finely chopped root ginger
1 T cornflour

Boil all ingredients for sauce except cornflour. Blend cornflour to a paste with a little water and stir into sauce. Serve on hot, sliced tongue.

OXTAILS

Ask the butcher to cut the oxtail into pieces between the natural joints. Oxtails may be braised, stewed or used in soups. Small tails are suitable for soups; 2 large tails should feed 6 adults when stewed or casseroled.

OXTAIL AND TOMATO CASSEROLE

Serves 6

3 medium onions, sliced
2 large carrots, sliced
2 T butter
2 large oxtails
1 T brown sugar
3 T flour
455 g can tomatoes, chopped
2 cloves garlic, crushed
2 sprigs parsley
½ t thyme
1 bayleaf
1 cup red wine
455 g can tomato soup
1 cup water
Salt and pepper

Melt butter in frypan and sauté vegetables until well browned. Remove from pan into a large casserole. Trim any excess fat from meat. Brown in pan and place in casserole. Sprinkle with brown sugar and flour. Add rest of ingredients to casserole.
  Bake 150°C for 3 hours. Cool and refrigerate overnight. Next day remove fat from top of casserole and reheat in oven (about 45 minutes).

MINCE MAGIC

Mince is one of the most versatile forms of meat. Not only beef, but pork, veal and lamb may be minced, allowing the meat to be cooked quickly in many ways. Beef topside is often available as a lean mince; chuck steak and trimmings make up the standard mince.

TASTY MEAT SAUCE

Serves 4
Serve over noodles, spaghetti, macaroni or rice. Prepare in bulk and store in meal-sized quantities in the deep freeze.

- **2 rashers bacon or 100 g bacon pieces**
- **2 medium onions**
- **1 medium carrot**
- **2 stalks celery**
- **50 g butter**
- **500 g minced beef**
- **½ cup dry white wine**
- **1½ cups beef stock**
- **¼ cup tomato purée**
- **¼ t ground nutmeg**
- **Salt, freshly ground black pepper**

Finely chop bacon, onions, carrot and celery. Melt butter in large heavy frypan. Add bacon and vegetables and sauté for 10 minutes, stirring often. Push mixture to one side and add meat. Fry until browned, stirring constantly.

Pour in wine, boil briskly for 1 minute and add stock and purée. Reduce heat and cook, covered, for 45 minutes, stirring occasionally. Season with nutmeg, salt and pepper. Serve with a crisp salad and hot bread.

FAVOURITE MEATBALLS

Serves 4
Quick to prepare. Use the oven to bake potatoes at the same time.

500 g minced beef
½ cup fresh breadcrumbs
½ t mixed herbs
Salt and pepper
1 egg
Flour

Sauce
1 cup tomato purée
¼ cup vinegar
2 T brown sugar
1 bayleaf
¼ t each ground ginger and nutmeg
½ cup water
1 medium onion, sliced

Combine meat with breadcrumbs, seasonings and egg. Roll mixture into balls and roll in flour. Place in lightly greased casserole. Mix all remaining ingredients for sauce in a saucepan. Bring to boil. Pour hot sauce over meatballs. Cover and bake 180°C for about 1¼ hours.

APRICOT GLAZED MEAT LOAF

Serves 6-8
Very attractive and a favourite with the family. Good with or without the sauce.

500 g minced beef
500 g sausage meat
1 cup fresh breadcrumbs
1 large onion, chopped
2 t curry powder
Salt and pepper
1 T chopped parsley

1 egg
½ cup milk
½ cup water
Apricot Sauce
220 g can apricots
¼ cup vinegar
2 T brown sugar

Combine mince, sausage meat, breadcrumbs, onion, seasonings, parsley and egg in a bowl. Beat well. Gradually add milk and water and continue beating until mixture is smooth. Shape meat into loaf and place in a large greased baking dish. Bake 180°C for 30 minutes.

To make sauce, place apricots, vinegar and sugar in a blender and blend until smooth (or pass through sieve). Simmer for 5 minutes. Continue baking meat loaf for a further hour, basting meat with sauce every 15 minutes. Serve hot or cold.

BEAN AND BEEF CASSEROLE

Serves about 4
A combination of minced beef, beans and cheese makes a high protein dish. Use less chilli powder if preferred.

1 medium onion, diced	2 t chilli powder
1 T butter	220 g can red kidney beans or similar
500 g minced beef	
½ t salt	2 cups potato crisps
1 clove garlic, crushed	100 g tasty cheddar cheese, grated
1 cup tomato sauce	
1 T white vinegar	

Sauté onion in butter until golden. Add beef and cook until brown and crumbly. Tip off any excess fat. Mix in salt, garlic, tomato sauce, vinegar and chilli powder. Cover and simmer 15 minutes. Add kidney beans.
   Place half meat mixture in the bottom of a deep casserole. Spread with 1 cup potato crisps and half the cheese. Place remaining meat on top. Finish with a layer of crisps then rest of cheese. Bake uncovered, 190°C for 30 minutes or until bubbly.

HERBED VEAL PATTIES

Serves about 4
Serve with sour cream which has been heated until just hot.

500 g minced veal	½ t salt
2 eggs	Freshly ground black pepper
4 T chopped parsley	2 T water
½ t dried basil	¾ cup dry breadcrumbs
½ t marjoram	Oil

Mix veal with 1 beaten egg, parsley, basil, marjoram, salt and pepper. Shape into 4 patties. (If minced veal is not available, buy stewing veal and mince as finely as possible.)
   Lightly beat second egg with water. Dip patties into egg mixture then into breadcrumbs. Refrigerate for at least an hour before cooking. Heat a little oil in large frypan and cook patties about 8 minutes each side, or until meat is no longer pink inside.

Lamburger

LAMBURGERS

Serves 6

The great NZ burger — don't overcook. Minced lamb may be from the leg or trimmed forequarter.

- 700 g lean minced lamb
- ¼ cup dry breadcrumbs
- 1 egg, beaten
- 1½ t ground coriander
- Grated rind and juice of ½ orange
- 2 T soy sauce
- 2 T oil

- 6 hamburger buns
- Lettuce
- Mayonnaise
- Tomato slices
- Onion rings
- Cucumber or orange slices
- Olives
- Parsley

Combine lamb, breadcrumbs, egg, coriander, rind and juice of orange, and soy sauce. Divide mixture into 6 equal parts and shape into patties. Heat oil in frypan and sauté patties about 4 minutes each side.

Meanwhile, heat 6 hamburger buns. Halve and butter thinly. Place a layer of lettuce and mayonnaise on the base, and 2 tomato slices. Top with meat patty, onion rings and slices of cucumber or orange. Place other half bun on top and garnish with olive and parsley, secured by a toothpick.

SERVING SAUSAGES DIFFERENTLY

There's always a place on the menu for sausages as they are popular family fare.

Sausages are a combination of ground beef, mutton and pork. Beef sausages are so named because they have more beef than mutton and pork. Soy bean flour or milk powder (protein) is also added to help bind the mixture.

To precook (or boil) sausages, place in warm water, then slowly bring to boiling point — the water should not bubble. The sausages should stand in this hot water for about 10-15 minutes.

SAUSAGE AND SULTANA CURRY

Serves 4
They will be back for more — serve on rice, noodles or potatoes.

- 2 T butter
- 6-8 beef sausages
- 2 medium onions, chopped
- 1 apple, peeled and chopped
- 1 T curry powder
- ½ cup sultanas
- 455 g can tomato soup
- ½ cup water
- ½ t beef stock powder
- Salt and pepper
- Chives

Melt butter — add sausages and cook gently until golden and cooked through. Remove from pan. Drain off excess fat leaving 1 T fat in pan.

Sauté onions until browned. Add apple and sauté a further minute. Stir in curry powder, cook 1 minute, then pour in sultanas, soup, water, stock and seasonings. Bring to the boil and simmer for 5 minutes. Add sausages and simmer a further 10 minutes uncovered. Garnish with chopped chives.

CHIPOLATA LOLLIPOPS

Serves 6
Fun food for the younger set.

- 500 g chipolatas in links
- 2 T butter, melted
- Tomato sauce

Bend 2 linked chipolatas round in a spiral shape to look like a lollipop. Spear with thin skewers about 20 cm long. Place cold water in wide frypan. Lie 'lollipops' flat in pan and slowly bring to boiling point. Remove from heat and allow to stand for 10 minutes. Drain.

Place skewered sausages on grilling rack. Brush with melted butter and place under preheated grill. Cook until just brown, turning once. Dip in tomato sauce and serve.

GARLIC ROLL

Serves 6-8
An appetising cold meat for salad days.

- 400 g sausage meat
- 200 g minced beef
- 100 g lean bacon or bacon pieces
- 2 cloves garlic, crushed
- ½ t mixed herbs
- 1 large hard-boiled egg, coarsely chopped
- 1 large fresh egg, beaten
- 1 cup fresh breadcrumbs
- Salt and pepper

Combine sausage meat and mince. Chop bacon finely and add to meat. Mix with all remaining ingredients.

On a well-floured board, form meat into a roll. Wrap neatly in muslin. Place in a steamer and cook over boiling water for 2 hours, turning occasionally. Leave to cool before removing muslin.

SAUSAGE SURPRISE

Serves 6
Grand for picnics. Prepare ahead and deep freeze.

- 3 rashers bacon
- 2 T butter or oil
- 1 small onion, chopped
- 150 g mushrooms, chopped
- 1 T each chopped parsley and mint
- Salt, freshly ground black pepper
- 400 g flaky pastry
- 6 precooked sausages
- Beaten egg for glazing

Grill bacon until crisp. Melt butter, sauté onion and mushrooms until soft. Remove from heat and add herbs and seasonings. Cool. Roll out pastry thinly and cut into 6 pieces about 13 cm square. Add chopped bacon to mushroom mixture and divide evenly over pastry squares.

Remove any skin from sausages and place sausages on top of mushroom mixture. Wrap one side of pastry over to meet the other. Seal and brush with beaten egg. Place on oven tray and bake 200°C for about 20 minutes, or until pastry is golden. Serve hot or cold with salad.

CREAMY SAUSAGE SALAD

Serves 6
Serve as a complete meal with crisp bread, or as part of a meal.

- 6 pork sausages
- 500 g potatoes
- ½ cup French dressing
- 1 medium onion, finely chopped
- 1 medium carrot, shredded
- 1 cup celery, finely chopped
- 220 g can pineapple pieces
- 2 T chopped parsley
- Salt, freshly ground black pepper
- ¾ cup mayonnaise
- ½ cup sour cream
- 1½ t prepared mustard
- Lettuce leaves
- Chopped parsley for garnish

Pan fry sausages until cooked. Set aside until cool. Peel potatoes and cook until just tender. Cut into dice while still warm and combine with French dressing. Stand for 1 hour. Combine onion, carrot, celery, drained pineapple, parsley, salt and pepper, and add to potato. Slice sausages into 5 mm rings and add to potato mixture.

Combine mayonnaise, sour cream and mustard. Fold into salad, mixing gently until vegetables and sausages are well coated. Place washed and crisp lettuce leaves on base of a salad bowl. Carefully spoon salad on top. Garnish with parsley.

SAUSAGE AND KIDNEY BEAN CASSEROLE

Serves about 4
A mixture of beans could be used to make this tasty dish. Serve with salad and hot rolls.

- 2 cups cooked red kidney beans
- 1 medium onion, chopped
- 1 green pepper, chopped
- 2 T butter
- 220 g can pineapple pieces
- 6 pork sausages
- 6 mushrooms or 2 rashers bacon, chopped or 6 slices cheese
- ½ cup brown sugar
- Salt and pepper

Spoon drained kidney beans into casserole. Sauté onion and green pepper in butter until soft. Mix into kidney beans, together with drained pineapple pieces. Reserve juice.

In frypan, cook sausages until browned and cooked through. Slit lengthwise and fill with sliced mushrooms, bacon or cheese. Place in casserole with beans. Drain excess fat from pan. Stir in brown sugar and reserved pineapple juice. Stir until sugar is dissolved and pour over sausages. Cover and bake 180°C for 50-60 minutes.

Sausage and Kidney Bean Casserole

PIES-A-PLENTY

Putting meat into crisp pastry is one of the oldest known methods of cooking. If you remember a few essentials while handling the pastry you will have a perfect pie every time:
- keep everything as cold as possible
- handle pastry lightly
- try not to stretch the pastry.

VEAL AND HAM PIE

Serves 6-8

An old-fashioned pie which lasts well for several days in the refrigerator — good for picnics or for summer buffets. Aspic is poured into the pie after it is cooked.

500 g boneless veal
225 g ham
2 T parsley, chopped
3 T chicken stock or water
½ t dried sage
½ t freshly ground black pepper
Hot water pastry (see p. 71)

3 eggs, hard-boiled
2½ t gelatine
2 t powdered chicken stock
1 cup boiling water
Beaten egg for glazing

Dice meat into 5 mm pieces. Place in bowl with parsley, stock or water, sage and black pepper. Mix thoroughly.

Take one-third of the pastry and set aside. Roll out remaining pastry to rectangle about 30 × 40 cm and 5 mm thick. Drape pastry over rolling pin and unroll over greased 23 × 13 cm loaf tin. Gently press pastry into base and sides of tin. Trim off excess pastry.

Spoon enough meat into pastry to half fill tin. Arrange hard-boiled eggs down centre. Cover with remaining meat. Roll reserved pastry into rectangle to cover top of pie. Trim excess pastry and crimp edges to seal pie. Cut a 3 cm vent in centre of pastry top. Use pastry scraps cut into shapes to decorate top of pie. Glaze top with beaten egg. Bake in centre of oven 200°C for ¾ hour, and 180°C for further ¾ hour, until top is golden. Cool for 15 minutes.

Meanwhile place gelatine and powdered stock into bowl; pour on boiling water and stir to dissolve. Pour mixture through funnel into opening of pie. Cool to room temperature and refrigerate for at least 6 hours. To serve, dip bottom of tin in hot water and invert onto plate. Cut in thick slices.

HOT WATER PASTRY

2½ cups plain flour
½ t salt
50 g lard

3 T milk
2 T water

Place flour and salt into a deep bowl. Melt lard with milk and water. Mix into flour a little at a time until flour can be gathered into compact ball. Knead until smooth then allow to rest in refrigerator for 30 minutes before using.

MEAT AND POTATO PASTRIES

Makes 4
Great for picnics — they can be served hot or cold, with salad.

350 g chuck steak
100 g raw potato
1 medium onion, grated
1 T tomato sauce

Salt, freshly ground black pepper
400 g crusty pie or shortcrust pastry
Beaten egg for glazing

Trim and cut meat and potato into 5 mm cubes. Place into bowl. Add sauce, salt, pepper and onion. Divide pastry into 4 equal pieces. Roll each piece into 20 cm circle.

Divide mixture into 4 and place in centre of pastry circles. Moisten edges with water. Bring edges of pastry together across top of meat mixture. Press edges together to seal. Pinch into flutes with fingers, then place on greased baking tray. Brush with egg and bake 220°C for 15 minutes then reduce temperature to 180°C and cook further 50 minutes.

STEAK AND KIDNEY PUDDING

Serves 6

The flavour is something to remember and well worth the extra work that this steamed pudding demands.

1 kg lean chuck or topside	1 bayleaf
225 g calf or lamb kidneys	150 g mushrooms, sliced
¼ cup flour	1 small onion, chopped
1 t salt	2 T finely chopped parsley
¼ t nutmeg	Suet pastry (see below)
Freshly ground black pepper	1¼ cups boiling water

Trim meat and cut into 3 cm cubes. Place in bowl with flour, salt, nutmeg, black pepper and crumbled bayleaf. Toss to coat evenly. Add mushrooms, onion and parsley. Roll out about two-thirds suet pastry into circle about 38 cm in diameter and about 5 mm thick. Drape pastry over 2-litre pudding basin. Gently press pastry into basin, being careful not to stretch it. Trim excess pastry. Roll out remaining pastry about 3 cm larger than basin top. Set aside.

Spoon meat into pastry-filled basin, filling it to within 1 cm of top. Pour in boiling water. Moisten pastry rim with water and place circle of pastry over meat. Crimp pastry all around with fork to seal it. Trim edges. Place double piece of greased foil over pudding, turning in edges to hold it in place. Dampen a clean teatowel and sprinkle with 2 T flour. Spread towel, flour side down, over top of pudding; tie with string just below rim of pudding basin. Tie diagonal corners of towel together, over top of pudding.

Place in large saucepan and pour in enough boiling water to come three-quarters of the way up side of basin. Bring to boil, cover and steam 5 hours. Add more water if necessary during cooking. To serve, lift pudding from water, remove towel and foil. Serve from basin or invert onto plate and slice like a pudding.

SUET PASTRY

225 g shredded suet, chilled	Freshly ground black pepper
4 cups self-raising flour	½-¾ cup icy water
1 t salt	

Place suet, flour, salt and pepper into large mixing bowl. Rub flour and fat until mixture is crumbly. Pour ½ cup icy water over mixture and gather into ball. If too dry, add more water 1 T at a time. Mixture should be fairly dry. Place on lightly floured board and knead lightly. Use immediately.

SATURDAY'S BEEF FLAN

Serves about 6
A can of corned beef, cottage cheese and eggs make up this tasty flan — serve hot or old.

- 1 medium onion, chopped
- 340 g can corned beef
- ½ t marjoram
- 400 g crusty pie pastry or similar
- 2 large eggs
- 1 cup cottage cheese
- Pepper
- 3 T chopped parsley

Combine onion, beef and marjoram. Roll out pastry thinly and line 23 cm flan dish. Place beef mixture in bottom. Beat eggs until frothy. Combine cottage cheese, pepper and parsley and fold into eggs. Mix well. Pour egg mixture over beef. Bake 1 hour at 190°C.

Left: Saturday's Beef Flan
Right: Veal and Ham Pie

CURRIES

A curry is a spicy eastern sauce usually containing meat or vegetables. Indian cooks mix their own spices for curries, according to preference and the food to be cooked. Commercial curry powders, available in our shops, are also a blend of spices. Inexpensive cuts of meat are usually used to make a curry and the long cooking time required to tenderise the meat also helps to mellow the flavours of the spices.

For entertaining, several curries may be served, each with a different flavour. They can be accompanied by rice, side dishes (or sambols), and chapatis, a bland Indian bread which complements the sharpness of the main meal.

TANGY BEEF CURRY

Serves 5-6
Not too hot — can also be cooked in a casserole.

800 g stewing steak
3 T flour
3 T sugar
Salt, freshly ground black pepper
2 t curry powder
2 t turmeric
½ t each mustard, ground ginger, mixed spice

3 T vinegar
3 T dry sherry
2 T tomato sauce
1 t Worcestershire sauce
¼ cup water
Grated rind and juice of 1 lemon
6 prunes, chopped

Cut meat into 3 cm cubes. Combine flour, sugar, salt, pepper, curry powder, turmeric, mustard, ginger and mixed spice. Mix well. Toss meat in this mixture and press seasonings well into meat. Stand for at least 2 hours.

Place meat into a heavy saucepan. Pour in remaining ingredients. Simmer over low heat for about 2 hours, until tender.

CURRIED VEAL ROLLS

Serves 4
Serve with or without the sauce.

4 veal schnitzels
2 bananas
2 t curry powder
Flour

Salt, freshly ground black pepper
Milk
Desiccated coconut
Butter

Cut schnitzels in half. Slice bananas lengthwise, then in half. Roll bananas in curry powder. Place piece of banana on each piece of schnitzel and roll up. Dip in seasoned flour, milk, then coconut. Press coconut in well.

Sauté gently in butter for about 15 minutes, turning occasionally. Serve accompanied by curry sauce (see overleaf).

Tangy Beef Curry

CURRY SAUCE

A useful sauce for sausages or cold meat as well.

- 2 T oil
- 1 small onion, diced
- 1 apple, peeled and diced
- 1-2 t curry powder
- 2 T flour
- ¾ cup coconut milk, or ¾ cup milk and ⅛ t coconut essence
- ½ t each salt and ground ginger

Heat oil. Sauté onion and apple. Stir in curry powder. Cover and cook 10 minutes. Add flour and stir until smooth. Add milk, essence, salt and ginger. Stir until thickened. Cover and simmer about 15 minutes.

LAMB — INDIAN STYLE

Serves 6

A true curry using a blend of spices.

- 1 kg boned lamb (or mutton) shoulder
- 3 cloves garlic, crushed
- 6 cardamom seeds
- ½ t each coriander, turmeric, ground cumin, cayenne pepper, ground ginger and salt
- 1 cup plain yoghurt
- 2 T butter
- 1 large onion, chopped
- 1 cup water
- Lemon juice
- ½ cup slivered almonds, toasted

Cut meat into 3 cm cubes. Combine all seasonings with yoghurt. Marinate meat in this mixture for several hours. Melt butter and sauté onion until transparent. Add meat and marinade. Cook 1 minute, then add water. Simmer, covered, for 30 minutes.

Uncover pan and simmer a further 30 minutes or until meat is tender and sauce thickened. Taste and flavour with lemon juice and more salt if necessary. Serve garnished with toasted almonds.

CURRIED FRUIT AND PORK

Serves 4
Substitute pineapple for tamarillos if desired.

2 T oil	2-3 t curry powder
1 medium onion, sliced	1 t salt
4 pork foreloin chops	2 T sultanas
4 T flour	1 T brown sugar
2 apples, chopped	4 tamarillos, skinned and sliced
1 banana, sliced	
1-1½ cups water	

Heat oil and lightly fry onion. Dredge chops in flour, then fry until brown. Transfer chops and onion to greased casserole. Add all remaining ingredients. Cover and bake 180°C for 1½ hours.

ACCOMPANIMENTS FOR CURRIES

Serve curries with at least three of the following: finely chopped pineapple, desiccated coconut, nuts, sliced raw onion, chopped cucumber, orange, banana, apples, kiwifruit, tamarillos, celery, hard-boiled eggs, pickles and chutneys. Serve in small bowls.

CHAPATIS

Makes 6

1 cup flour	½ t salt
1 cup wholemeal flour	¾ cup warm water (approx.)

Sieve flour and salt. Add enough water to make stiff but pliable dough. Divide dough into about 6 pieces. Roll out thinly to size and shape of a pancake.
    Melt a little butter in frypan. Fry one chapati at a time. Cook until bubbles appear then turn and cook until golden. Best served warm.

MAKING THE MOST OF LEFTOVERS

Cold lamb and cucumber pickles are a treat. But with a little imagination, leftovers can also be transformed into something hot and exciting. Remembering that they should look as good as they taste, leftover meats can be served as spicy rice, in fancy pastry cases or in fashionable casseroles.

MEAT IN A CASE

Serves 3-4
Pastry or 'vol-au-vent' cases are great for leftover meats and vegetables combined with a small tin of soup and some seasonings.

400 g flaky pastry
340 g can cream of chicken soup
1 t Worcestershire sauce
½ t tarragon
1 cup leftover pork, lamb or veal, diced
½ cup cooked rice (optional)
1 cup diced vegetables, e.g. carrots, corn, peas, asparagus, mushrooms
Beaten egg for glazing

Roll pastry to 1.5 cm thickness. Cut out two 15 cm circles. Brush oven tray with water and place one circle on it. Cut 10 cm circle from centre of second round. Place rim on moistened circle on tray — it should fit perfectly. Press down lightly on rim and score in diamond pattern. Refrigerate 15 minutes.

Brush top with beaten egg. Bake 220°C for 10 minutes then reduce to 190°C for about 30 minutes until shell is well risen and brown. (This may be kept in an airtight container for a few days or in the deep freeze.)

To make filling, heat soup with sauce and tarragon. Pour it over meat and vegetables and reheat all ingredients slowly. If pastry case is cold reheat in oven. Fill with meat mixture and serve.

ENCORE LAMB

Serves about 3
A mixture of lamb, mushrooms, peas, herbs and sauces are served over rice.

1 rasher bacon, chopped
1 large onion, sliced
1 t sugar
50 g mushrooms, sliced
2 T butter
1 t Worcestershire sauce
2 T tomato sauce
¾ cup yoghurt
1 cup frozen peas
¼ t dried tarragon
150 g cooked lamb, thinly sliced

Sauté bacon until crisp. Push to one side then sauté onion until transparent. Add sugar. Melt butter in pan and sauté mushrooms until soft.

Add sauces, yoghurt, peas and tarragon. Cover and cook over very low heat for about 10 minutes. Add lamb and heat through thoroughly. Serve on hot rice, with crunchy salad.

Meat in a Case

SPICY RICE

Serves 4-6

A colourful dish that deliciously disguises last night's leftover meat.

- 2 cups raw rice
- 2 T butter or oil
- 2 onions, thickly sliced
- ½ t turmeric
- 1 t whole peppercorns
- 4 cloves
- ¼ t cinnamon
- 4 cups hot water
- 3 t powdered chicken stock
- ½ cup sultanas
- 1-2 cups cooked pork or beef, finely diced
- 4 eggs, hard-boiled
- 1 cup cooked green peas
- Almonds

Wash rice, drain and dry. Heat butter, sauté onions until golden. Add spices, stir, then add rice. Stir fry until golden. Pour in water and chicken stock. Mix well. Simmer gently, covered, for 15-20 minutes. After 10 minutes, add sultanas and meat. Do not stir.
   Before serving, fluff up rice with fork. Transfer to serving plate. Garnish with eggs cut in half, hot peas and almonds which have been fried in a little butter or oil until golden.

PORK AND APPLE BAKE

Serves about 5

Leftover roast pork and raw apple is covered with gravy and mashed kumara.

- 2-3 cups diced cooked pork
- 2 tart apples, peeled and sliced
- 3 T brown sugar
- ¼ t mixed spice
- ¾ cup leftover gravy
- 3 medium kumaras
- 3 T butter
- ¼ cup creamy milk
- Salt and pepper
- Nutmeg

Lightly grease a 20 cm casserole. Add meat and apples. Sprinkle with brown sugar, mixed spice, and pour gravy over. Cook kumara and mash with butter, milk, salt and pepper. Spread evenly over meat mixture. Sprinkle with a little nutmeg. Bake, uncovered, at 180°C for 45 minutes.

HAM AND BACON

There is no question about it — smoky flavoured bacon and juicy pink ham are always mouth-watering.

Traditionally, ham is a cured leg of pork while bacon is cut from the loin and foreloin. Curing is one of the oldest methods of preserving. Today advanced techniques allow a milder and sweeter method of curing than the heavily salted meats of yesteryear. The meat is pickled or corned with a solution of salt and water (brine) and then it is smoked.

Bacon is cured in a similar way to ham but because the cuts used are thinner than the leg, bacon tends to have a more smoky flavour. Bacon from the loin is called side bacon and has a strip of fat down the side. Middle bacon is from the middle of the loin. Bacon from the foreloin is called shoulder bacon and is very lean. In recent years the foreloin (or forequarter) of the pig has been boned, rolled, lightly cooked and used as boiling bacon.

There is very little waste from the carcass of a pig — even the rinds of bacon make delicious snacks if baked in a hot oven for 10-15 minutes until they are crisp. The rinds can also be used to flavour stews and soups.

PREPARING A HAM

Everyone loves a festive ham! They are equally good at formal dinners or at casual beer parties. They may be purchased cooked or uncooked, with bone in or out.

Hams may be cooked in a variety of ways. If preferred they may be soaked for several hours or overnight in cold water to remove some of the salt. The ham cure these days is generally mild. Remove skin after cooking.

Oven-bag ham: pre-soak ham then place in an extra large oven bag. Add 2 cups water, an onion and some peppercorns. Tie about 8 cm away from meat. Make 3-4 holes in bag with prongs of carving fork. Place in roasting dish. Bake 160°C for 25 minutes per 500 g. Let cool a while before removing from bag.

Boiled ham: place ham in large pan with cold water to cover. Add a few peppercorns, a sprig of parsley and a bayleaf. Bring slowly to boil and simmer 20 minutes per 500 g. Cook 15 minutes per 500 g if ham is over 5 kg. Allow to cool in liquid.

Dough case: pre-soak ham. Mix sufficient flour and milk or water to make a very thick paste to cover entire ham. It must be sufficiently thick all over to keep in any juices. Place ham in roasting pan. Cook 200°C for 15 minutes then reduce heat to 160°C for 25 minutes per 500 g. Remove crust and skin.

GLAZING A HAM

Score fat into squares or diamonds about every 3 cm. Place ham in large baking dish. Glaze with any of the following. Bake 180°C for about 30 minutes.
- Spread about ½ cup marmalade over ham. Baste occasionally.
- Blend ¾ cup brown sugar, 1 T dry mustard and 3 T cornflour — mix to thick paste with sherry. Spread over ham and bake.
- Mix 1 cup brown sugar with sufficient pineapple juice to make thick paste. Spread over ham and baste occasionally.

Decorate glazed ham with cloves, glacé cherries and pineapple rings if desired.

BOILING BACON

Boiling bacon is very similar to ham but its flavour is a little stronger. Cuts used for boiling are from the foreloin, the hand (shoulder) or the hock. They may be simmered in water and served hot or cold. The foreloin may be purchased boned and rolled. The weight of pieces available for boiling range from 1.3 kg to 2.25 kg.

Soak bacon in cold water to cover for at least 6 hours. Drain. Slowly bring to boil in fresh water. Simmer slowly allowing 25 minutes per 500 g. If it is to be served hot, remove rind, slice and serve with mustard or pineapple sauce.

If it is to be served cold, allow to cool in liquid. Remove rind and roll in dry breadcrumbs. Boiling bacon may also be glazed in a similar manner to ham if preferred.

APPLE AND BACON HOCK CASSEROLE

Serves 6

Rich but scrumptious — 1 bacon hock usually has enough meat to serve 2 people.

- **3 large bacon hocks**
- **12 small whole onions, peeled**
- **3 tart apples, peeled and sliced**
- **1½ t dry mustard**
- **1 T brown sugar**
- **Freshly ground black pepper**
- **1¼ cups cider or apple juice**
- **½ cup sultanas**

Soak hocks in cold water to cover for at least 6 hours. Drain. Place in a deep baking dish or casserole. Add onions and apples. Combine mustard, sugar and pepper with cider or apple juice. Pour over ingredients in casserole. Sprinkle sultanas over.

Cover and bake 160°C for 2-2½ hours. Remove meat from bones

while still hot and return to casserole. Thicken if desired with a little flour and water paste.

Boiling Bacon

HAM STEAKS

Often cooked and served with pineapple and brown sugar, ham steaks are a tasty treat. They are cut from:
- the leg of an uncooked ham — these are called gammon steaks
- a boned and rolled shoulder bacon — these give a uniform result
- a boned, rolled and cooked leg of ham.

Pan fry in a little butter or oil until golden each side.

Ham Steaks

HAWAIIAN HAM STEAKS

Serves 4

4 ham steaks cut at least 1.5 cm thick
2 T brown sugar
⅜ cup pineapple juice
4 T butter

Slit rind of steak at about 3 cm intervals. Combine sugar and pineapple juice — dip steaks into this mixture. Heat butter in heavy pan and sauté steaks until golden on both sides, turning frequently. Cooking time is about 5 minutes each side for raw gammon steaks (cut 3 cm thick) and 3 minutes each side for others. When cooked, remove to serving platter.

Stir pineapple juice and sugar into pan and heat through. Pour over steaks. Serve with creamed potatoes, sautéed pineapple rings and a crisp salad.

HAM AND VEGETABLE TEA

Serves 6
A popular lunch or tea dish. An ideal way of using up those little leftover pieces from the festive ham.

- 2 eggs, beaten
- 450 g can cream-style corn
- 450 g can mixed vegetables, drained, or 2 cups frozen mixed vegetables
- 1 cup soft breadcrumbs
- 1 small onion, finely chopped
- 1 t dry mustard
- Salt and pepper
- ¼ t oregano
- 2 cups diced cooked ham (about 200 g)
- 220 g can sliced mushrooms in sauce
- ½ cup dry breadcrumbs
- 2 T butter

Combine egg, corn, mixed vegetables, breadcrumbs, onion, mustard, salt, pepper and oregano. Carefully stir in ham and mushrooms.

Turn into a 6-cup, greased casserole. Sprinkle with dry breadcrumbs and dot with butter. Bake, uncovered, 180°C for 50-60 minutes or until heated through.

BACON 'N' PEARS

Serves 4
A quick and different slant to breakfast.

- 4 pears
- 4 rashers bacon

Cut pears in half lengthwise, and remove stems and cores. Cut rashers of bacon in half. Place bacon pieces over top of each pear half.

Arrange pears in shallow baking pan and bake 200°C for 20-30 minutes or until pears are soft and bacon is crisp.

CONTINENTAL MEATS

Exploring continental meats is an adventure.

The frankfurter is often served between a bun with pickle or mustard. It is a cooked and smoked sausage like the lesser known rookwurst and thuringer. These tasty sausages should, like saveloys and polonies, be cooked before eating, by standing in very hot water (not boiling) for about 20 minutes.

The making of continental sausages, especially salami, can be likened to the making of cheese. Fresh beef, and sometimes pork, salt, spices and herbs are combined. Some salamis are dried in a humidity chamber for several weeks, allowing the flavours to blend and mature. Others are smoked for 2-3 days. Salamis are meant to be thinly sliced and served cold — but they do make good toppings for pizzas. Salamis come in a range of flavours and sizes too. Like smoked beef, they can be wrapped around pineapple, gherkins, asparagus spears or cottage cheese.

Continental meat loaves, such as liver loaf, balleron and choritzo are ideal picnic foods, and they can also be sliced, sautéed and served hot. They may also be dipped in egg and breadcrumbs before frying.

RED CABBAGE CASSEROLE WITH ROOKWURST

Serves 4
A hearty meal for the whole family — serve with boiled potatoes.

- ½ medium red cabbage
- 2 T butter
- 1 onion, chopped
- 2 apples, peeled and sliced
- 3 T white vinegar
- 3 T water
- 2 T sugar
- Freshly ground black pepper
- 4 rookwurst

Shred cabbage finely, place in large saucepan of boiling water. Boil 1 minute then drain. Melt butter in saucepan and fry onion until soft. Add apples and cook 1 minute.

Place layer of cabbage in greased casserole. Cover with layer of onion and apple. Continue layers, sprinkling with vinegar, water, sugar, and pepper between each layer. Cover with greased foil. Bake 160°C for ¾ hour. Uncover and tuck in the 4 rookwurst. Cover again and bake a further ¾ hour.

Red Cabbage Casserole with Rookwurst

VIENNA FONDUE

Serves 4-5

A very satisfying fondue — it cooks quickly too.

500 g selection of continental meats, e.g. salami, pepperoni kabanosy, frankfurters, balleron loaf	225 g Colby cheese (or other soft cheese) Oil

Place sliced salami, cubed sausages and cubed cheese on plate in an attractive manner. Half fill fondue pot with oil. Heat until a cube of bread will brown in less than a minute. (This can be done on the range then transferred to the spirit burner.)

Spear a cube of cheese, then a cube of sausage or slice of salami on fondue fork. Place in hot oil until cheese begins to melt. Transfer to dinner plate, and, using another fork, dip it in sauce and eat it.

Serve with at least 3 sauces, e.g. horseradish sauce, mustard sauce (2 T prepared mustard combined with ½ cup mayonnaise) or a fruit sauce (plum or apple). The fondue may also be accompanied by pickled onions, French bread and a crisp salad.

PEPPERONI PIZZA

Serves 6-8

Base
1¾ t dried yeast
¾ cup warm water
¼ t sugar
2 cups flour
½ t salt
2 T oil

Topping
½ cup tomato purée
1 medium onion, sliced
100 g cheese, thinly sliced
2 pepperoni cabanossi
Parsley

To make base, sprinkle yeast on warm water, stand 2 minutes then stir in sugar. Leave in warm place until mixture starts bubbling.

Place flour and salt in bowl and stir in oil. When yeast mixture is ready, stir into flour. Mix well, then knead until shiny. Place in greased bowl, cover and leave in warm place until doubled in size (about 1 hour). When risen, pat out to fit base of 30 cm pizza pie tray.

Spread with tomato purée and onion. Position cheese slices over this then top with diagonally sliced pepperoni. Bake 180°C for 20-25 minutes. Sprinkle with parsley and serve.

SWEET 'N' SOUR FRANKFURTERS

Serves 4

Add a small tin of pineapple chunks if desired. Good on rice.

- 1 small onion, finely chopped
- ½ cup tomato sauce
- ½ cup water
- ½ t salt
- 1 T brown sugar
- 1 T vinegar
- 1 T prepared mustard
- ½ t chilli powder
- 8 frankfurters
- Spring onions, chopped or 1 green pepper, chopped

Place all ingredients except frankfurters into saucepan. Simmer gently, uncovered, for 5 minutes. Score frankfurters diagonally at 3 cm intervals. Add to sauce. Cover and simmer gently 5 minutes longer or until heated through. Sprinkle with spring onions or green peppers and serve.

SOUR CREAM BRATWURST

Serves 4–5

Tasty, rich, easy to prepare.

- 4 bratwurst
- 2 T butter
- 4 T warm water
- 2 t flour
- ¼ t salt
- Freshly ground black pepper
- ½ cup sour cream

If bratwurst are not cooked, place them in large saucepan of very hot water and let stand for 10 minutes. Drain and pat dry. Melt butter in large, heavy frypan. Gently sauté bratwurst until golden. Add water, reduce heat and simmer, uncovered, for 15 minutes. Turn occasionally and add more water if necessary.

Stir flour and seasonings into sour cream. Carefully add to frypan. Stir on low heat for about 3 minutes. Bratwurst may be served whole with sauce or sliced into 5 mm rounds. Serve with boiled potatoes and cabbage salad.

PINEAPPLE AND SALAMI SALAD

Serves 2-4
Could be served in individual salad bowls as a complete lunch.

225 g selection sliced salami
100 g cheddar cheese
450 g can sliced pineapple

1 small lettuce
¼ cup **French dressing**

Cut salami into quarters and cheese into small cubes. Cut drained pineapple into thirds. Wash lettuce and crisp in refrigerator. Tear lettuce and place in base of salad bowl.

Combine salami, cheese and pineapple and sprinkle with French dressing. Place on top of lettuce. Toss just before serving.

Free flow chops and casseroled meat in foil container (see *Home Freezing and Storage*)

HOME FREEZING AND STORAGE

Freezing is the best known method of preserving meat. It is thought that freezing may tenderise meat but this does not mean that a piece of braising steak may be grilled after it has been frozen! Whether buying half a sheep or a family roast, meat for the freezer should be high quality and well packed.

BUYING IN BULK

Approximate weights:
- side of beef   135 kg
- side of veal   45 kg
- side of pork   18 kg
- whole lamb   14 kg
- whole hogget   20 kg

From a side of beef you could expect approximately:
9.5%   grilling steak
23.0% stewing steak
23.0% roasts and corned meat
8.0%   minced beef
4.0%   sausage meat
4.5%   kidney, oxtail, suet
28.0% fat, bone and waste

If there are certain portions that the family will not eat, it may be better to purchase an assorted meat pack or take advantage of weekly specials, rather than purchase a whole carcass.

Selecting a carcass
Choose a high quality carcass, not too fat, not too lean. Excess fat may become rancid, extra lean meat is inclined to dry out. There should be sufficient fat or marbling between the tissues to prevent the meat from drying out.

Aging
A freshly slaughtered carcass should be hung in a chiller or refrigerator at 5°C to improve texture and flavour — this is called aging or conditioning. As a guide: beef needs to age for at least 5 days, veal and pork 1 day, lamb 1-2 days, and mutton 2-4 days.

METHODS OF FREEZING

Large cuts: trim off excess fat, bone and roll roasts if possible to save freezer space. If bones are left, pad any sharp points, which could pierce packaging material, with wad of foil or paper.
Small cuts: 'free flow' if possible. Place one layer of steaks, chops,

schnitzels, patties or sausages on metal or plastic tray. Position uncovered tray in coldest part of freezer (next to walls) for up to an hour only. Remove solid meat into a large plastic bag or other container. Seal, tie and replace in freezer. Meat will remain 'free flowing' — individual chops, however many are required, may be removed without having to thaw out the rest. Small cuts may also be kept separate with a double layer of plastic. Old plastic bags cut into squares are suitable. Place a pile of chops, separated by plastic, into plastic bag and seal. Schnitzels may be egg and breadcrumbed first.
Stewing cuts: these may be cubed and packaged in meal-sized quantities.
Minced meat: when buying a side of beef, some of it will be minced. Bulk packs of veal, lamb and pork may also include mince. There are many quick and tasty ways to prepare this meat — some can be found in the mince recipe section of this book. Flat packages of meat are easier to store — lie bag of mince on level surface and pat gently so that it forms a flat patty shape rather than a round ball.

PACKAGING

Choose good quality packaging materials that are airtight, odourless, greaseproof and strong. Plastic bags and tin foil are the most common materials used.

Excess air must be removed from plastic bag — either squeeze out or use a vacuum pump. These are simple to operate and can be bought in most food or hardware shops. Tie bags, preferably with paper- or plastic-covered metal ties. Food, especially meat, will dry out in the freezer if it is not packed in airtight and moisture-proof bags or containers. Sometimes food looks as if it is burnt. This is 'freezer burn'. Loss of food value and moisture leaves the food with little flavour. Freezer air can also turn fat rancid.

Once meat is frozen, it is easy to confuse fillet steak with topside! Label each parcel with the amount, the type of meat and the date. Adhesive labels and masking tape are suitable — write details in ballpoint pen.

MAXIMUM STORAGE LIFE

Recommended Maximum Storage Life at -18°C (in months)

beef, lamb, hogget	9-12
veal, pork	4-6
minced meat (not pork)	3
seasoned minced meat	1-2
sausage meat (unseasoned)	3
sausages (pork)	1-2

bacon (slab)	3-4
bacon (sliced)	1
ham (uncooked slab)	3-4
ham (cooked)	1-2
corned cuts	1-2
variety meats (not liver)	3
liver	1-2

FREEZING COOKED MEATS

Most cooked meats freeze well. It is a recommended means of dealing with meat left over from the weekend roast, besides being an ideal way to economise on time and effort by preparing meals in large quantities. These can be divided into meal-sized quantities and frozen for a later occasion.

Hints
- Food flavours tend to intensify in the freezer, so it is advisable to minimise spices and herbs in dishes to be stored for a long period.
- Frozen gravies and sauces thickened with plain flour separate and run on reheating. Either use 'rice flour' or 'ground rice' in place of flour for thickening, or take a little flour or cornflour, mix to a paste with water and add to the cold gravy just before freezing.
- A high standard of hygiene is important. Cool foods quickly prior to freezing to prevent any chance of food poisoning.
- Surplus fat shortens storage life, so remove extra fat from meat dishes before freezing.

Roast meats
If meat is to be served cold or used in a reheated dish, pack into an airtight bag, remove air and seal. Storage time: 1 month.

If meat is to be served hot, place slices in foil dish or casserole. Pour on gravy to cover. Cover with foil, label and freeze. Reheat in oven 200°C for about 1 hour or in saucepan over low heat. Storage time: 4 months.

Casseroles and stews
- Freeze in casseroles either lined or unlined. If lined with foil or plastic, the meat, once frozen, can be lifted out of the casserole, wrapped and placed back in freezer. (Choose a casserole with straight sides though!) To reheat frozen meat still in casserole dish, place in cold oven, turn to 200°C and cook until heated through (about 1 hour depending on size).
- Freeze in foil dishes.
- Freeze in plastic containers, leaving 3 cm headroom for expansion of liquid during freezing. Meat may be reheated in saucepan over low heat. Storage life: 4 months.

Meat pies
Freeze before or after baking. Storage life: baked pies 1 month, unbaked pies 2 months. Prepare unbaked pie as usual, but do not vent the top pastry layer. Wrap and freeze. To bake, cut vents in pastry top, bake, unthawed, for 20 minutes at 200°C then 190°C until cooked. Baked pies may be thawed at room temperature or in oven 190°C.

Meat loaves
Freeze before or after baking. If it is to be served hot, there is little advantage cooking meat loaf first, as reheating will take about half the time it would to bake. Storage life: 1 month.

THAWING MEAT

Meat thawed slowly retains many more of its natural juices — thawing in the refrigerator gives the best results. If, however, time is short, thaw quickly by placing meat, in its wrapping, in frequent changes of cold water, or place in front of a cold fan. A microwave oven can also be used.

Approximate thawing times for meat:
- in a refrigerator, 6 hours per 500 g
- at room temperature, 3 hours per 500 g
- before a fan or in cold water, ½-¾ hour per 500 g
- in microwave, roasts about 10 minutes per 500 g (see manufacturer's instructions).

COOKING FROZEN MEATS

Meats may be cooked satisfactorily from the frozen state. However large cuts (roasts) need about 20 minutes per 500 g extra cooking time. It is recommended that, to obtain uniform cooking, larger cuts be partially thawed before cooking.

Frozen chops, sausages and schnitzels need to be cooked only a few minutes longer than fresh ones. If possible, allow steaks to thaw before cooking.

HINTS ON REFRIGERATOR STORAGE

Wrap meat *loosely* in waxed paper, foil, plastic film or muslin. During storage a certain amount of air should be allowed to circulate around the meat.

Recommended Maximum Storage Life at 2-10°C

roasts	5-7 days
steaks	3-5 days
chops	3 days
stewing meats	2 days
minced meat	2 days
sausages	2 days
variety meats	2 days
home-cooked meats	2-3 days
bacon	7 days
hams (whole)	1-2 weeks
hams (sliced)	4-5 days
luncheon (sliced)	3-4 days
unsliced luncheon chubs e.g. Bologna	4-6 days

GLOSSARY

International recipes often use cuts with which we are not familiar. Because other countries process their animals in different ways, comparable cuts are not available here. This list includes the nearest possible substitute available from our butchers.

BEEF

aitch bone *silverside (usually corned)*
baron of beef *double loin of beef*
beef steak *thickflank or bolar*
bolar *thick end of blade from shoulder — sold in 1 piece for pot roasting*
butt steak *silverside cut from a young animal — not corned — pan fry*
clod *shin*
club steak *from middle of carcass — grill*
entrecôte (ribsteak) *rib eye or scotch fillet*
eye fillet *cut from middle of fillet*
fillet mignon *piece of fillet trimmed to round shape*
foreshank *gravy beef cut from foreleg*
ground beef *mince*
hamburger beef *mince*
minute steak *thin pieces of steak put through steak cubing machine to break fibres — grill quickly*
New York Cut *sirloin steak*
oyster blade *cut from shoulder of young carcass — grill*
oyster steak or popes eye *taken from topside — grill*
porterhouse *sirloin steak*
saddle of beef *rump and loin of beef*
scotch fillet or cubed roll *taken from under ribs*
T-bone *porterhouse on bone*
tenderboy steak *rump steak pounded in criss-cross fashion (crosscut blade sometimes used)*
tenderloin *whole fillet*
top round *thickflank*
top rump *first cuts off flank — only for casseroles*
tournedos *piece of fillet trimmed to a round shape*
undercut *part of fillet from under rump*
wing rib roast *1-3 ribs off rib bone carcass*

VEAL

cutlets *boneless — cut from loin*
escalope, scallop, scaloppine, schnitzel *thin slices of veal from flank*

or sirloin
fillet *topside, bolar or thickflank — roast*
knuckle *shank*

LAMB

best end of neck *6-7 rib chops nearest neck*
chump chops *chops cut from fillet end of leg*
crown roast *2 racks of lamb joined*
lamb steaks *cut from chump or boned leg of lamb*
noisettes *boned and rolled loin of lamb — cut into round steaks*
rack of lamb *6-7 rib chops. Chined (backbone removed), trimmed and left in 1 piece*
raised shoulder *shank end of shoulder or forequarter — a small roast*
saratoga roll *boned and rolled loin of lamb, tied and left whole*
scrag end *neck*
rosettes *round neck chops*
schnitzels *cut from boned leg of lamb*
shank *knuckle*
spanish neck *thick end of forequarter or best end neck*

PORK

cushion or blade *foreloin*
fillet of pork *half-leg of pork taken from chump end*
hand *part of breast and foreleg — usually corned*
hock *foreleg*
pork fillet *long tender portion of boneless meat taken from inside of loin*
pork fingers *finger-like cuts from the belly*
salt pork *corned or pickled pork*
schnitzels *thin, boneless slices of pork from boned shoulder, rib end of loin or boned leg*
spareribs *use pork fingers*
speck *pork fat*
spring *belly*
steaks *from chump end of leg*
traditional *one of two sizes at which pigs are processed. Traditional porkers weigh about 30-40 kg*
trim *the bigger size at which pigs are processed (60-70 kg). A wider variety of cuts gained from trim porkers*

CUTS OF TRADITIONAL PORK

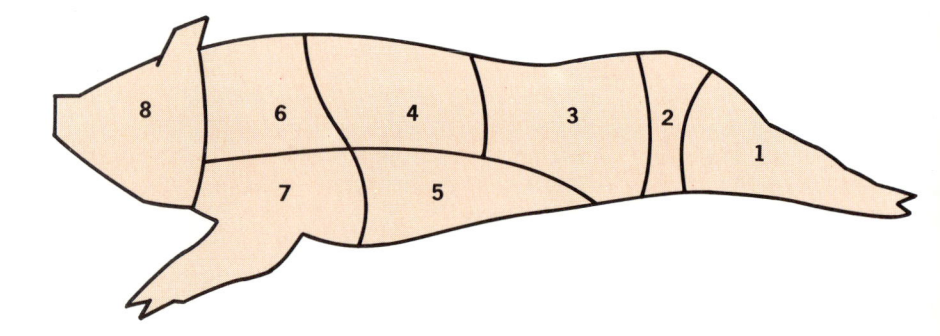

1 leg, shank *roast, corned, pickled*
2 leg, fillet *leg or chump chops*
3 loin *rolled roast, loin chops, pork fillet underneath*
4 rib loin *rib roast, crown roast, rib chops*
5 belly (spring) *pork fingers, pork pieces, rolled roast, pickled*
6 foreloin (cushion) *foreloin chops* ⎫
7 hand *pickled* ⎬ **forequarter**
8 head ⎭

CUTS OF TRIM PORK

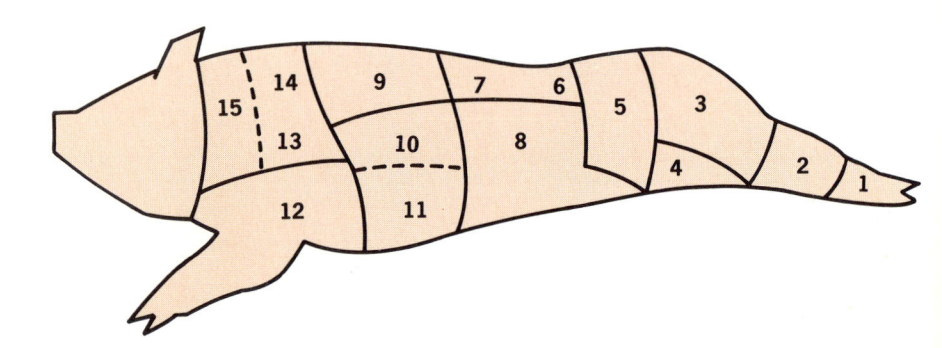

1 trotter
2 hamhock *boil, pieces*
3 silverside/topside *roast, steak*
4 schnitzels
5 rump *roast, steak*
6 butterfly steaks
7 midloin steaks
8 rolled roast
9 pork medallion (rib loin)
10 spareribs
11 bacon
12 hand (rolled roast)
13 Y-bone steaks
14 scotch fillet *roast, steak*
15 shoulder roast

CUTS OF LAMB (HOGGET, MUTTON)

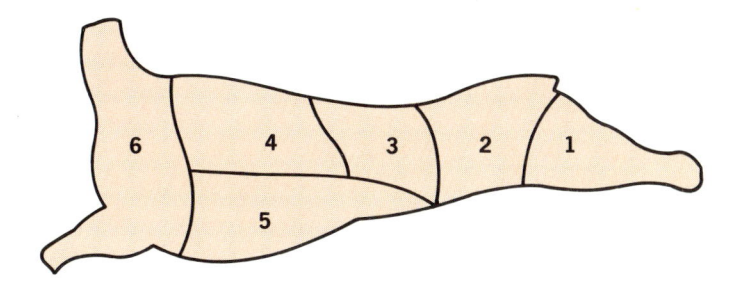

1 leg, shank end
2 leg, fillet end *roast, chump chops, leg steaks*
3 middle loin *roast, loin chops, noisettes*
4 rib end loin *roast, rack of lamb, crown roast, cutlets*
5 flap *stewing pieces, rolled roast*
6 forequarter *shoulder roast, shoulder chops, best end neck, scrag end*

CUTS OF BEEF (VEAL)

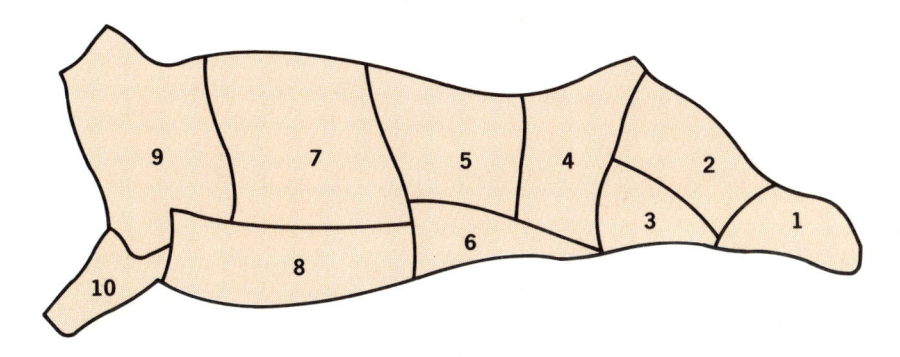

1 leg *gravy beef*
2 silverside *topside underneath*
3 thick flank
4 rump *fillet underneath*
5 loin *sirloin, T-bone*
6 flank *thin flank, skirt steak*
7 ribs *rolled rib roast, rib steaks, scotch fillet underneath*
8 brisket *usually corned or rolled*
9 blade *bolar roast, blade steak, chuck underneath*
10 shin (foreshank) *gravy beef*

INDEX

A

Accompaniments
  Barbecues 51
  Curries 77
  Roasts 28
Apple and Bacon Hock Casserole 82
Apricot Glazed Meat Loaf 62

B

Bacon
  Boiling 82
  Casserole with Beef and Oysters 20
  Hock and Apple Casserole 82
  'n' Pears 85
  with Tripe and Tomatoes 57
  with Veal Cutlets 30
Barbecues
  Accompaniments 51
  Barbecued Luncheon 51
  Marinated Skewered Veal 51
  Mixed Kebab Platter 50
  Outdoor Pork 48
  Piha Lamb 50
  Soy and Ginger Steak 48
Basil Butter 47
Bean and Beef Casserole 63
Beef
  Apricot Glazed Meat Loaf 62
  Bacon and Oyster Casserole 20
  Casserole, Bean and 63
  Bolar Pot Roast 11
  Cuts 99
  Dad's Meat Loaf 17
  Favourite Meatballs 62
  Garlic Roll 67
  Lager 9
  Meat and Potato Pastries 71
  One-pot Dinner 21
  Paper-thin Pepper Steaks 35
  Peppered Rump Steak 32
  Perfect Pan-fried Steaks 34
  Pot Roast 15
  Potpourri 52
  Ribbons 38
  Roast, Rare Rump 24
  Roast, Spiced Rolled 26
  Saturday's Flan 73
  Soy and Ginger Steak 48
  Steak and Kidney Pudding 72
  Tangy Curry 74
  Tasty Meat Sauce 61
  and Tomatoes 42
Blue Cheese Butter 51
Boiling Bacon 82
Bolar Pot Roast 11
Brain Savoury 55
Braised Pork in Soy Sauce 10
Bratwurst, Sour Cream 89
Brawn 8
Buying in Bulk 91
Buying Meat 5

C

Canterbury Mutton 8
Chapatis 77
Chipolata Lollipops 66
Chops
  Citrus Braised 12
  Garlic Pork 54
  Lamb, with Herbs 15
  Savoury Lamb 53
  Soya Lamb 19
Chow Mein, Veal 42
Citrus Braised Chops 12
Country-style Pork 21
Crackling, Pork 28
Creamy Sausage Salad 68
Crusted Veal Kebabs 40
Curry
  Accompaniments 77
  Fruit and Pork 77
  Sauce 76
  Sausage and Sultana 66
  Tangy Beef 74
  Veal Rolls 74
Cuts
  Beef 99
  Hogget 99
  Lamb 99
  Mutton 99
  Pork, Traditional 98
  Pork, Trim 98
  Veal 99

D

Dad's Meat Loaf 17
Dill Pot Roast 54

E

Encore Lamb 78

F

Favourite Meatballs 62
Flan, Saturday's Beef 73
Fondues
  Lamb and Cheese Ball 46
  Mixed Meat 45
  Vienna 88
Frankfurters, Sweet 'n' Sour 89
Freezing Methods 91

G

Garlic
  Leg of Lamb 25
  Pork Chops 54
  Roll 67
Glossary 96
Gravy 28

H

Ham
  Boiled 81

Dough Case 81
Glazing 82
Hawaiian Steaks 84
Oven-bag 81
Preparing 81
Steaks 84
and Veal Pie 70
and Vegetable Tea 85
Hearts 58
　Mock Steak and Kidney Pie 58
Herbed
　Lamb Shanks 12
　Liver Pâté 59
　Veal Patties 63
Hogget
　Canterbury Mutton 8
　Citrus Braised Chops 12
　Cuts 99
Honeyed Pork Fingers 32
Horseradish Cream Whip 46
Hot Water Pastry 71

Kebabs
　Crusted Veal 40
　Mixed Platter 50
　Pohutukawa Lamb 31
Kidney 58
　Mock Steak and Kidney Pie 58
　Steak and Kidney Pudding 72
Kidney Bean Casserole, Sausage and 68

Lager Beef 9
Lamb
　and Cheese Ball Fondue 46
　Chops with Herbs 15
　Citrus Braised Chops 12
　Cuts 99
　Encore 78
　Garlic Leg 25
　Herbed Shanks 12
　Indian Style 76
　Lamburgers 65
　Lemon Crumbed Cutlets 39
　Noisettes 35
　Piha 50
　and Pineapple 20
　Pohutukawa Kebabs 31
　Roast Leg 16
　Rolled Seasoned 27
　Savoury Chops 53
　Soya Chops 19
　Steaks with Capers and Cheese 37
Lamburgers 65
Lemon Crumbed Cutlets 39
Liver Pâté, Herbed 59
Luncheon, Barbecued 51

Marinated Skewered Veal 51
Meat and Potato Pastries 71
Meatballs, Favourite 62
Meat in a Case 78

Meat Loaf
　Apricot Glazed 62
　Dad's 17
Mince
　Bean and Beef Casserole 63
　Favourite Meatballs 62
　Garlic Roll 67
　Herbed Veal Patties 63
　Lamb and Cheese Ball Fondue 46
　Lamburgers 65
　Meat Loaf, Apricot Glazed 62
　Meat Loaf, Dad's 17
　Pork Fritters 40
　Tasty Meat Sauce 61
Mixed Kebab Platter 50
Mixed Meat Fondue 45
Mock Steak and Kidney Pie 58
Mushrooms, Sweetbreads with 56
Mustard Sauce 46
Mutton
　Canterbury 8
　Cuts 99
　Ham 7

Noisettes, Lamb 35

One-pot Beef Dinner 21
Onion Sauce 47
Outdoor Pork 48
Oxtail and Tomato Casserole 60
Oyster Casserole, Beef, Bacon and 20

Paper-thin Pepper Steaks 35
Pastry
　Hot Water 71
　Meat and Potato 71
　Meat in a Case 78
　Suet 72
Pâté, Herbed Liver 59
Pears, Bacon 'n' 85
Peppered Rump Steak 32
Pepperoni Pizza 88
Perfect Pan-fried Steaks 34
Pickled Pork with Mustard Sauce 9
Piha Lamb 50
Pineapple
　and Lamb 20
　Pot Roast 11
　and Salami Salad 90
Pizza, Pepperoni 88
Pohutukawa Lamb Kebabs 31
Pork
　and Apple Bake 80
　Braised in Soy Sauce 10
　Chops, Garlic 54
　Country-style 21
　Crackling 28
　and Crunchy Vegetable Bake 22
　and Fruit, Curried 77
　Cuts, Traditional 98
　Cuts, Trim 98
　Fritters 40

101

Honeyed Fingers 32
Loin, Roasted 27
Outdoor 48
Pickled with Mustard Sauce 9
Schnitzel with Fruity Sauce 36
Sweet 'n' Sour 16
with Stir Fried Rice 44
and Vegetables 41
Potpourri 52
Pot Roast
  Beef 15
  Bolar 11
  Dill 54
  Pineapple 11
Pressed Tongue 60

Rare Rump Roast 24
Red Cabbage Casserole with Rookwurst 86
Refrigerator Storage, Hints 95
Rice
  and Pork, Stir Fried 44
  Spicy 80
Roast
  Accompaniments 28
  Beef, Spiced Rolled 26
  Leg of Lamb 16
  Pork Loin 27
  Rump, Rare 24
Rolled Seasoned Lamb 27
Rookwurst and Red Cabbage Casserole 86
Rosemary Veal 26

Salad
  Creamy Sausage 68
  Melon and Cucumber 51
  Pineapple and Salami 90
  Spinach 51
Salami and Pineapple Salad 90
Saturday's Beef Flan 73
Sauce
  Curry 76
  Fruity 36
  Horseradish Cream Whip 46
  Mustard 46
  Onion 47
  Spicy Orange 60
  Tasty Meat 61
Sausage
  Garlic Roll 67
  and Kidney Bean Casserole 68
  Salad, Creamy 68
  and Sultana Curry 66
  Surprise 67
Savoury Lamb Chops 53
Sour Cream
  Bratwurst 89

Veal 19
Soy and Ginger Steak 48
Soya Lamb Chops 19
Spiced Rolled Roast Beef 26
Spicy Rice 80
Steak
  Ham 84
  and Kidney Pie, Mock 58
  and Kidney Pudding 72
  Lamb, with Capers and Cheese 37
  Perfect Pan-fried 34
  Paper-thin Pepper 35
  Rump, Peppered 32
  Soy and Ginger 48
Stir Fried Rice and Pork 44
Suet Pastry 72
Sultana Curry, Sausage and 66
Sweetbreads with Mushrooms 56
Sweet 'n' Sour
  Frankfurters 89
  Pork 16

Tangy Beef Curry 74
Tasty Meat Sauce 61
Temperatures 6
Thawing Meat 94
Tomato Casserole, Oxtail and 60
Tomatoes, Beef and 42
Tongue 59
  Pressed 60
  with Spicy Orange Sauce 60
Tripe 56
  with Bacon and Tomatoes 57

Veal
  Apricot and Banana Casserole 14
  Chow Mein 42
  with Cream Sauce 36
  Crusted Kebabs 40
  Curried Rolls 74
  Cutlets Stuffed with Bacon 30
  Cuts 99
  Dill Pot Roast 54
  and Ham Pie 70
  Herbed Patties 63
  Marinated Skewered 51
  Pineapple Pot Roast 11
  Rosemary 26
  Sour Cream 19
Vegetables in Foil 51
Vienna Fondue 88

Weights and Measures 5

Yorkshire Pudding 28